If I Could Find That Church

If I Could Find That Church

Seeking a Biblical Church for Today's World

Toby Morgan

Book Editor: Wanda Griffith
Editorial Assistant: Tammy Hatfield
Copy Editor: Oreeda Burnette

Library of Congress Catalog Card Number: 2003103175
ISBN: 0-87148-391-2
Copyright © 2003 by Pathway Press
Cleveland, Tennessee 37311
All Rights Reserved
Printed in the United States of America

Dedication

This book is dedicated to my darling wife,

Diane,

without whom I would be lost in this world.
My love for her grows with each passing year!

To my sons,

Stephen and Andrew.

Like the apostle John stated so long ago,
I have no greater joy than to know you
walk with God in a mighty way.

To the wonderful saints of the Pathway congregation:
You give me the inspiration to write and preach.
Your willingness to seek to become
"that church" amazes me!
Thanks for your devotion to seek the face of God
with a passion to follow His plans!

Contents

Foreword

Toby Morgan pastors the exciting Pathway Church of God in Mobile, Alabama. He writes from his experiences as a pastor and has discovered a problem that transcends church cultures, mind-sets and social consciousness. It is an age-old question of the identity of the church, its perception and its performance. The author makes the statement that "God never changes; on the other hand, God is never the same." This profound theme runs throughout this book and, if read and applied, could change the direction of any church.

Many churches have become program-driven and stagnant. They exist only to please a certain group, or even worse, to preserve a particular way of "having church." *If I Could Find That Church* deals with the problems, ruts and lethargy of the 21st-century church; however, it does not stop there. This book brings out in a unique way the Scriptural solution and remedy to make your church that kind of church—a church the world needs and God wants.

It is obvious that the Holy Spirit has inspired Pastor Morgan. He pens these pertinent prescriptions for a church to become relevant and able to cope with our changing world. Everyone would like to find a church where Jesus Christ is proclaimed as Lord—where people are valued as God's creation, where programs are adjusted to fit our day, and where worship is true and heartfelt. You are in for an informative, convicting, exciting read.

Thank you, Toby Morgan, for being sensitive to the Lord and practical in approach. I pray that we can develop the kind of church that people will desire to attend.

—Joseph Mirkovich

Introduction

For too long, many of us in the local church have been working feverishly to provide answers to questions no one is asking. Trapped in models that soared at one time, we now bear a close resemblance to a Model T Ford that is trying to keep up with the powerful cars roaring around racetracks at 200 miles per hour. Something has to change!

It is no secret that God is moving around the world. Outside the U.S. and in Europe, the greatest revival of all time is coruscating like a Christmas tree. One recent statistic released by missiologists revealed that every day some 122,000 people are baptized into Christ! Think of it . . . every day this earth is experiencing more than 40 Pentecosts! That makes me want to shout! The Lord is truly preparing His bride!

However, in my nation and in the nations of Europe, not much is happening. The spiritual growth statistics are virtually nugatory. The leaders of the local church must rise up and do something. It's time to sharpen the saw and become all God wants us to be. The day is almost spent, night is about to fall when none of us will be able to work (see John 9:4). My call, my heart, is for my church, and yours, to become "that church"—the church that makes a difference in the lives of as many people as possible.

My prayer for you as you read this book is for the Holy Spirit to birth in you such an intense desire to become "that church," that one year from now you will be experiencing the greatest outpouring of the Holy Spirit, the most phenomenal revival, the most intense growth pains you have ever dreamed possible. May the Lord make it happen in my church and yours!

"We ought always to thank God for you, brothers, and rightly so, because your faith is growing more and more, and the love every one of you has for each other is increasing" (2 Thessalonians 1:3).

The Missing Church

O ne of the most compelling stories I have ever read is related by Tony Campolo in his book *The Kingdom of God Is a Party.* This story embodies the very essence of the meaning and purpose of the church. I seldom read the story without being moved to tears by its captivating meaning. Unlike other forms of communication—a song, a poem or even a movie—this tale has not lost its edge of demonstrating the reason Christ left us on the earth.

While on a speaking trip to Hawaii, Campolo was walking late one night, actually early in the predawn morning, when he happened upon a diner that stayed open 24 hours a day. While eating a dough-nut and drinking some coffee, a number of prosti-tutes came in.

Campolo found himself in the midst of a large

group of loud prostitutes, not exactly the comfort zone for ministers. He overheard a conversation between two of the women: "Tomorrow's my birthday. I'm gonna be 39." The response was less than enthusiastic. "So whaddaya want . . . a party?"

"Nah, why do you have to be so mean? I don't expect a party. I've never had one before. Why should I have one now?" said the first.

When Tony heard that, he made a decision. When the women left, he asked the owner if the one who was having a birthday came in every night.

"Yes, that's Agnes. She comes in every night." So Tony and the owner made arrangements to bring decorations, bake a cake and show up at 3 a.m. the following day. They outfitted the diner with a sign that said "Happy Birthday, Agnes" and hung crepe paper everywhere. The word was spread. By 3:15, the place was filled with prostitutes and Tony Campolo.

At 3:30, the door swung open and in walked Agnes. Tony had everyone yell, "Happy Birthday, Agnes!" He says he's never seen anyone so flabbergasted, so stunned. Agnes' mouth fell open. By the end of the song, Agnes' eyes had filled with tears. When the birthday cake with all the candles came out, she openly cried. Everyone yelled, "Blow out the candles, Agnes." But she couldn't. "Cut the cake, Agnes," they continued, but she couldn't. Looking at the cake,

Agnes said, "If it's OK, I'd like to keep the cake a little while."

Agnes left with the cake, saying, "I'll come back—honest I will." So Agnes slowly took her cake down the street a couple of doors, carrying it like a ring on a pillow.

When the door to the diner closed, there was silence. Tony says he wasn't sure what to do, so he said, "What do you say we pray?" He prayed for Agnes, for her salvation, for her life to be changed, and for God's goodness to touch her. When Tony finished, the owner leaned over the counter and said, "Hey, you never told me you were a preacher. What kind of church do you belong to?"

Tony said, "I belong to a church that throws birthday parties for whores at 3:30 in the morning."

The response of the owner of the diner is the clincher. Listen to his words: "No you don't. There's no church like that. If there was, I'd join it. I'd join a church like that!"

The words of that diner owner speak prophetically to the church today: *If I could find a church like that, I'd join it.*

He was addressing all who really want to be a part of the last-day harvest. His message is loud and clear . . . there are people in the harvest who will come to Christ if we will only make a way for them to come in!

Some would run to a church where they can find

love and acceptance. After all, everyone is looking for love and acceptance. We long for, even crave, such a haven in our lost and hurting world. When the church really becomes the body Christ intended, hurting and straying people will find a safe haven and will come pouring in.

Providing Real Answers

It's time the church wakes up to a startling revelation . . . *the hurting world couldn't care less about all our belief systems!* They are desperately searching for something to get them through the tedium of next week's meetings, seeking something to soothe the aching pain caused by their kids who have gone astray, frantically groping for something—anything to keep their family together. They simply aren't concerned about all the *stuff* over which the average church gets so bent out of shape.

When a church finally realizes that and starts caring— starts providing the real answer through the power of God and loving friendship, people will run through its doors!

Of course, some will rail against just such a church. When any church starts to make an inroad into the harvest field around it, there will be an abundance of religious "protectionists" who will uncover a million and one problems with it. Ignoring the fact that people are being saved and added to the kingdom of God, critics point out such glaring insufficiencies as these:

- They will let anybody in that church!

- They have no standards over at that place!

- They are just doing that for numbers!

- If they really preached truth, they wouldn't have all those new people!

I guess the bottom line is this: We are tough on things that don't bother us and are "gun-barrel" straight on those things with which we do have a problem. Perhaps my idea of the church is misinformed, but from what I can see of Jesus, our primary purpose on this planet is to be a place where those who are hurting can come and find a refuge.

After all, didn't Jesus use the parable and say, "The sick are the ones who need a physician" (see Matthew 9:12)? If that is true, why should it bother anyone when a church becomes a place of healing? Don't let it bother you. They labeled Jesus a "friend of sinners." If He could stand the insult, so can we!

Incredibly, some people will ruin such a church. Rushing in to be sure all is done "decently and in order," they will impose their standards over the lives of all who come. In an effort to root out the undesirable elements of the body, a move of God will cease and people will be hurt in the name of making the church a respectable place where people feel comfortable.

Now is the time we step back and take a close look at how this whole church business got started in the first place. I can't find much respectability about the cross . . . not much refinement in the brutal way the Romans put men to death. I find no merit in stripping a man naked, beating him until his flesh, bone and blood becomes a spectacle, then nailing him to some wood to die a lingering and excruciating death. Yet, that is precisely how the church in which you and I participate every Sunday had its genesis.

Discarding Old Ideas

Could it be remotely possible that God has brought us to the place where we need to discard our ideas of what appeals to men and, in their place, seek what pleases Him? Isn't that what we are really supposed to be doing anyway?

I think the answer to both questions is yes. I also contend that when any church reaches such a status, people will want to discover the amazing quality exuding from that church. When they come, the Holy Spirit will do His work and they will be saved! Actually, I get excited thinking about the possibilities of striving to become the kind of church that restaurant owner said didn't exist.

One of Paul's churches, the church at Thessalonica, appears to have been such a church. Paul esteemed them

very highly. He even bragged about them in his writings
to them. They probably weren't all they could have been,
but not many churches ever reach that status. However,
they were a church that made inroads into the harvest
around them. Take a moment to consider how Paul
boasted about them:

> Paul, Silas and Timothy, To the church of the
> Thessalonians in God our Father and the Lord Jesus
> Christ: Grace and peace to you from God the Father and
> the Lord Jesus Christ. We ought always to thank God for
> you, brothers, and rightly so, because your faith is grow-
> ing more and more, and the love every one of you has
> for each other is increasing. Therefore, among God's
> churches we boast about your perseverance and faith in
> all the persecutions and trials you are enduring (2
> Thessalonians 1:1-4).

Paul found some endearing qualities in that group of
believers that must serve as the foundations of our
churches today if we are going to be effective and relevant to our culture. These qualities work regardless of
the situation or location of a church. If believers will
simply espouse what the Thessalonian church implemented, they can make a difference in the lives of
those who come in contact with them. What qualities
am I referencing?

They Were Loyal

Paul lauds the church in Thessalonica for its patience

21

and faith in the face of persecution and tribulation (v. 4). The members of that body were hanging in there during some pretty tough times. In an earlier letter, the apostle gave us a glimpse into some of the pressures they were experiencing.

> For you, brothers, became imitators of God's churches in Judea, which are in Christ Jesus: You suffered from your own countrymen the same things those churches suffered from the Jews, who killed the Lord Jesus and the prophets and also drove us out. They displease God and are hostile to all men (1 Thessalonians 2:14, 15).

They were already being persecuted by the Jewish authorities, and the Romans weren't far behind. As a matter of fact, some of them were under such duress they thought they had missed the Rapture and were already living in the Day of the Lord.

Paul sought to quell their fears by exhorting them to not be easily shaken:

> Concerning the coming of our Lord Jesus Christ and our being gathered to him, we ask you, brothers, not to become easily unsettled or alarmed by some prophecy, report or letter supposed to have come from us, saying that the day of the Lord has already come (2 Thessalonians 2:1, 2).

What's really amazing about this church was the fact that in spite of their fears about missing the Rapture and the pressure being put on them because of their faith, they were remaining loyal to Christ! Here they were, catching it from Satan and fearing all along it was coming from God; worried they had missed the second coming of the Lord and were entering the terrible Tribulation . . . *and they kept right on doing what they knew to do!* That, my friend, is loyalty!

They Persevered

I love the word *perserverance* Paul used in 1:4 to convey the idea of enduring. It goes far beyond some of the ideas we have fostered like, "Hold the fort 'til Jesus comes." It means the manly continuance of what you are supposed to be doing when the pressure is really on. For us today, it means continuing in loyalty to Jesus Christ, doing what only the church can do in the face of fearful opposition.

The looming forces of darkness are gathering on the horizon in ways we have never witnessed. Face it, we are living in a society that will cheer you for standing up for what you believe, just as long as you don't believe in Jesus Christ or the Bible.

Not long ago, the United States Attorney General John Ashcroft was pilloried in the news media. His heinous misdeed? He was holding a Bible study and prayer group in his office before office hours! Anyone would think the scandal-laden previous administration would have awakened a desire in the American public for something other than sexual misconduct and the heavy-handed use of force against religious groups. But no, the attorney general caught days of media-vented lava because he had the temerity to read the Bible and pray with people in his office.

That's one tiny example of the dramatic shift away from God in our nation. I believe it will get worse as time goes by. I foresee a day when so many chaotic voices clamor for attention, the church will be shoved so far into the background it will be of no use or value. *That is, unless we rise above our enemy and become a church that has power with God and cares for nothing more!*

The church that remains loyal to the calling God has given will never be defeated! It may go through so many changes those of us active in the church today won't recognize it, but God's church—the loyal church—will survive!

Our First Loyalty Is to Save Souls

It isn't true that *we* save anyone, Jesus does that. Our job is to see that it is done. The church has the message of hope that cuts deeper than any surgeon's scalpel. This truth can probe deeper than any therapist can dig, look further inward than any scientist can gaze. No one else has the message of the church of Jesus Christ—no one.

Simply put, that message says we are sinners in bondage, but Jesus Christ can set us free.

⌂ Washington isn't going to spread that word.

⌂ State politicians aren't going to spread that word.

⌂ The NAACP isn't going to spread that word.

⌂ The Christian Coalition isn't going to spread that word.

⌂ Political parties aren't going to spread that word.

⌂ Charitable organizations aren't going to spread that word.

⌂ Only the church of Jesus Christ is going to shout it from the housetops, "Jesus Saves!"

If we are going to touch the hearts of people in our hardened day, we must remain loyal to our message. One reason the world has ignored us is because we are trying to say what they can hear elsewhere. If we make the mistake of becoming another Rotary Club, we will lose because the Rotary serves a meal and meets at a more convenient hour!

No, our task must be singular. In all we do, whether it is a Christmas pageant, a program honoring senior citizens, a church dinner, whatever, it must press us toward telling someone about the great news of the freedom found in Jesus.

Our Second Loyalty Is to Stop Satan

We are in a battle with an ancient foe. We must never forget that. While the sociologists, psychologists and behaviorists are standing around scratching their heads in amazement, wondering why on earth kids take guns and shoot their classmates at schools, we have some understanding. While they suggest the reason is easy access to guns, those who understand God's timeline know better.

You can believe what you want, but we have always had access to guns in our country. Growing up in a small town in Alabama, hunting and participating in other outdoor sports, I have had access to firearms all my life. My father's generation had access to weapons galore. But neither their generation nor mine ever thought about taking a gun to school and shooting the place up because someone did or said something we didn't like.

What Makes the Difference Today?

It's easy to assign blame. Look at the following passages of Scripture.

> The Spirit clearly says that in later times some will abandon the faith and follow deceiving spirits and things taught by demons (1 Timothy 4:1).

> For the time will come when men will not put up with sound doctrine. Instead, to suit their own desires, they

will gather around them a great number of teachers to say what their itching ears want to hear. They will turn their ears away from the truth and turn aside to myths (2 Timothy 4:3, 4).

First of all, you must understand that in the last days scoffers will come, scoffing and following their own evil desires (2 Peter 3:3).

The church understands Satan is having a heyday and the only institution devoted to stopping his pernicious plan happens to be the church. That's why we must—simply must—stand in the gap and use all the power given us by the Lord to halt Satan's carnage-filled advance.

It's time the churches of today revert back to the tactics used in the Book of Acts. You won't find them marching against the social ills of the day. Nowhere do we read where they ever marched against the corrupt government of Rome.

No, they understood the demonic powers behind the evil of their day and attacked in the places where they had power. They used prayer, loving people even when they were unlovable, accepting people as they were, depending on the power of the Holy Ghost to make a difference. All these same ways to dislodge Satan are still available to us today. What worked for them will work for us if we will allow God to fully have His way in our lives.

Salt to Society

Jesus taught us the absolute importance of being relevant to our society. All our flashy programs and multimillion dollar buildings won't accomplish one thing if we fail to bring in the lost. It's time the church realizes afresh our assigned task of carrying our message outside our walls as the Scripture says:

> "You are the salt of the earth. But if the salt loses its saltiness, how can it be made salty again? It is no longer good for anything, except to be thrown out and trampled by men. You are the light of the world. A city on a hill cannot be hidden. Neither do people light a lamp and put it under a bowl. Instead they put it on its stand, and it gives light to everyone in the house. In the same way, let your light shine before men, that they may see your good deeds and praise your Father in heaven" (Matthew 5:13-16).

Salt has little value if it is only used to occupy space in a cupboard. Likewise, the church has little value if all we are going to do is come into a place to worship, have a good time, then leave and never be poured out in the dying world around us.

The church is the only entity that can do what has to be done. Until Jesus comes, we must be busy in His work. We must remain loyal to our Lord and Savior, boldly proclaiming His worth, honor and delivering power. God will pour out His Spirit upon such a church. People are searching for such a church.

A Church Led by the Spirit

Paul boasted about more than loyalty. The church in Thessalonica was being led by the Spirit of God. Note his commendation of their progress in following the leading of the Holy Spirit:

"We ought always to thank God for you, brothers, and rightly so, because your faith is growing more and more, and the love every one of you has for each other is increasing" (2 Thessalonians 1:3).

Many churches are loyal today. They open their doors every Sunday. They have a Sunday school. They have a youth program. They have children's classes. They have some type of ladies ministry, and a few even manage to assemble several men and call it a men's ministry. But, aside from these busy activities, there is nothing happening in the Spirit. No one is getting saved. No one is ever filled with the Spirit. No one gets healed or changed by the power of God.

Many churches today are similar to a large steam engine locomotive in a Michigan museum. Mounted beside the mammoth piece of machinery is a plaque that reveals that 96 percent of the power generated by the massive steam engines was used in moving the locomotive. Only 4 percent of the power generated was used to pull the load.

What a picture of many modern churches. Ninety-six percent of all we do is just to keep us going . . . the saints, that is. Only 4 percent of our efforts constitute pulling others into the fold. If we are not careful, we will all fall into a terrible trap. It's deceptive and deadly. The results are devastating. The trap? It is a subtle, but debilitating practice of striving so hard to please ourselves that we create such a monster of debt and inbred programs that we have nothing left with which to reach out to the lost.

I believe the church at Sardis had fallen prey to this same situation. Remember what Jesus had to say to them? He could, in all likelihood, say the very same words to many churches today.

> "To the angel of the church in Sardis write: These are the words of him who holds the seven spirits of God and the seven stars. I know your deeds; you have a reputation of being alive, but you are dead. Wake up! Strengthen what remains and is about to die, for I have not found your deeds complete in the sight of my God. Remember, therefore, what you have received and heard; obey it, and repent. But if you do not wake up, I will come like a thief, and you will not know at what time I will come to you. Yet you have a few people in Sardis who have not soiled their clothes. They will walk with me, dressed in white, for they are worthy" (Revelation 3:1-4).

The people in the Sardis church had many things going for them; unfortunately, being led by the Spirit of God wasn't one of them. But that one thing is really all that matters!

Resistance to Change

For most of us, the problem is not desiring the Holy Spirit to lead us, it is our mulish resistance to any change the Holy Spirit might want to bring in our deeply entrenched patterns of action. If you want to follow the Holy Spirit, you must be willing to change.

It has often been said that insanity is repeating the same action and expecting a different result each time. The bitter truth is that if we keep on doing the same things we have done in the past, we will continue to get the same results. Nowhere is change more needed than in the church, and nowhere is the change more vehemently resisted than in the church.

I heard of a woman who once said to her pastor, "Reverend, if God were alive today, He would be shocked at the way our church has changed!" That's the point. God is alive and God is a God of change! I know, it's a paradox. On the one hand, God is forever the same. We sing and preach the fact that God never changes. Yet here I am, positing the opposite. Does that make me a heretic?

No. I am in no way insinuating God changes in His nature or makeup; rather I am declaring that God constantly changes His methods. Think about it for a moment. Those in the Word of God who followed the lead of the Holy Spirit, both Old and New Testament saints alike, discovered a broad range of diversity in the way God worked.

⌂ One time God had His people win a victory by marching around a city silently for six days, then having a concert and shouting on the seventh.

⌂ Another time God had the same people go behind a smaller town and sneak up on the inhabitants.

⌂ Still another time, God had them dig a ditch around an altar, fill it with water and offer prayer before He sent fire and hailstones.

⌂ Then God had them go on a recruitment trip through the nation and gather everyone who could handle a spear or sword.

⌂ God had Gideon winnow the numbers down to a paltry 300 or so men.

Same God, Same Nation, Different Methods.

For many of us, the problem is illustrated by the statement of the pastor whose church was struck by lightning. When the people asked what they were going to do, he responded, "It's OK. We are insured around here against acts of God."

He nailed us! On many fronts, we are inoculated against any move of God. We have become so entrenched in our own ways, so obstinate in our own predictable patterns, that a real move of God is next to impossible. We need to wake up and realize how desperately we need Him. Then we must cry out, "God, make us pliable in Your hands once more!"

For this very reason, make every effort to add to your faith goodness; and to goodness, knowledge; and to knowledge, self-control; and to self-control, perseverance; and to perseverance, godliness; and to godliness, brotherly kindness; and to brotherly kindness, love. For if you possess these qualities in increasing measure, they will keep you from being ineffective and unproductive in your knowledge of our Lord Jesus Christ (2 Peter 1:5-8).

2

A Welcoming Church

It was a large church, by most standards. My family, Diane and our two sons, Stephen and Andrew, were guests on a Sunday morning in a very productive church. There were approximately 500 adults in the worship center along with approximately 200 children and workers who were busy in other areas of the church.

The pastor and staff were wonderful people. The pastor preached a fine message. The singing was excellent and the church seemed to respond to the moving of the Holy Spirit. The facilities were modern and expensive. Yes, this was a "happening" place to be on Sundays. Yet, with all those things going for it, the most prominent thing etched in my mind about that Sunday morning was the fact no one spoke to us. That's right, no one.

And it wasn't due to a lack of fellowship time or the encouragement from the platform to "be friendly and greet someone." All those things took place, but not one person bothered to speak to this family of four who was visiting for the first time. As you can imagine, had we been looking for a church home, that one would have had to go a long way in order for us to even consider a return trip. Making people feel welcome is a vital part of any church that wishes to grow.

In his efforts to assist the churches of his day, the apostle Peter gave some straightforward commands, linked with a powerful promise, which address the glaring need for a church to be a place of welcome for all who enter.

> For this very reason, make every effort to add to your faith goodness; and to goodness, knowledge; and to knowledge, self-control; and to self-control, perseverance; and to perseverance, godliness; and to godliness, brotherly kindness; and to brotherly kindness, love. For if you possess these qualities in increasing measure, they will keep you from being ineffective and unproductive in your knowledge of our Lord Jesus Christ (2 Peter 1:5-8).

Isn't it amazing that brotherly kindness is ranked with self-control? Not a devoted believer alive would dispute the need for Christians to live lives of measured control that reflect the power of the Holy Spirit. Yet, for some reason we seem to think we, as Christians, can treat individuals with emotions ranging from lack of concern to outright contempt.

Added Strength

The apostle, under the heavy influence of the Holy Spirit, strikes at our nonchalant attitude with the promise of strength and stability to those who add brotherly love to our lives. He tells us this addition to our spiritual lives will give us added strength. What a promise! Grow strong in the Lord . . . grow strong in a loving attitude toward others, and you will never fail!

Apparently, many within the church haven't implemented this strength into daily living. How can we be so sure of this promise? A simple comparison of the promise with the product will reveal whether or not we are strong in the Lord.

In his challenging book, *ChurchNext: Quantum Changes in How We Do Ministry,* Eddie Gibbs points out some glaring truths about the state of today's church that lead to one conclusion: *Many churches are failing!* Consider these statistics:

1. In 1968, the United Methodist Church in North America had 41,901 congregations with a total membership of 10,990,720 people. By 1995 those numbers had shrunk to 36,361 churches and 8,535,662 members.

2. The average member of a mainline church is over 50 in age while the average American is in their 30s.

3. If the present trends continue, up to 60 percent of all existing Christian congregations will disappear by the year 2050.[1]

The sad truth is that thousands of churches close their doors every year. Each time the lights are turned off for the last time, the presence of Jesus in a community is diminished. And all this is happening during a time when Americans are deeply interested in spiritual matters. As a matter of fact, regardless of how it is spun by the media, surveys reveal that a majority of Americans want *more,* not less religion.

A recent poll from Public Agenda, a secular think tank, showed that most Americans feel society would improve if people were more devout in their religious lives. A poll of more than 1,500 people showed that 69 percent of Americans felt more religion is the best way to strengthen moral behavior and family values. A whopping 74 percent felt it is a bad idea to raise children without any religion.[2]

We Are Not Doing Something Right

We are in the middle of a field that is "white [and ready] to harvest" (John 4:35, KJV). But we seem to be losing ground on so many fronts in the church.

It's time for us to be brutally honest with ourselves and come face-to-face with the fact that we are not doing something right. We have all the methods, technology, manpower and money we could ever need. We have tools that members of the first-century churches never dreamed possible. Still, in this country, we seem to be fighting a losing battle with the rising tide of post-Christian era morality and thinking.

I am convinced that one of the reasons we are in such a fight for our lives in the church is the unseen, but very real, shield we have erected that says to the outside world, "If you aren't like us, you aren't welcome here."

Our attitudes must change to implement the idea of Jesus that says the world is the harvest field and the church is here for merely one purpose—*to reap the harvest set before us.*

This Is Not About Us

In one church I pastored, I conducted a survey among the people. Several hundred questionnaires were completed and turned in. What I found was not shocking, since I had read many surveys, but it was alarming because I thought this church was different. The first question was simple enough: "What do you consider the first priority of the church?"

The overwhelming answer (nearly 85%) was, "To

take care of the members of the church." Only about 5-7 percent of the respondents felt the main priority of the church was to win the lost.

I am afraid the major reason we are failing to reach the lost men and women around us is because of the pernicious attitude that pervades the American church today. When we allow this spirit to prevail in our churches and become so self-absorbed that everything revolves around meeting our needs, it is no wonder we lose sight of the Great Commission. After all, if I can go to church, link up with some family and friends, have my emotional needs met, and possibly get something from the Lord that helps me through the upcoming week, why should I worry if someone else needs God? My needs are met and that's all that matters!

That goes against everything Jesus stands for. Remember, all who call themselves Christian profess to follow Jesus. We are in varying degrees of commitment, but we all want to follow His example. Here is His spin on what He is all about:

> For the Son of Man came to seek and to save what was lost (Luke 19:10).

> "What do you think? If a man owns a hundred sheep, and one of them wanders away, will he not leave the ninety-nine on the hills and go to look for the one that wandered off ? And if he finds it, I tell you the truth, he is happier about that one sheep than about the

ninety-nine that did not wander off. In the same way your Father in heaven is not willing that any of these little ones should be lost" (Matthew 18:12-14).

Jesus called them together and said, "You know that the rulers of the Gentiles lord it over them, and their high officials exercise authority over them. Not so with you. Instead, whoever wants to become great among you must be your servant, and whoever wants to be first must be your slave—just as the Son of Man did not come to be served, but to serve, and to give his life as a ransom for many" (20:25-28).

Friend, this is not about us. Those of us who know the Lord and have set our eyes on heaven are important to Jesus. But He calls for us to turn our eyes away from our needs and focus instead on the needs of others. After all, He has already promised to meet our needs.

The most important need is for people to feel welcome and really wanted. I am convinced that church attendance will reverse and revival will once again sweep the nation when the church demolishes the invisible wall that says to people on the outside, "When you get like us, you can come in."

If we can do a good enough job of breaking down those barriers, we will have to do some hasty construction. We won't have enough church pews to hold the people who will clamor to become part of a church that makes them welcome and puts them in touch with Almighty God.

If the church is not about us, just whom is it for? Whom are we supposed to be concerned about? Whom are we supposed to welcome? How do we welcome people?

These are legitimate concerns for any church that is serious about touching the harvest of God. As far as I can discern, there are three kinds of people we will encounter. It is imperative for each one to find a place of warm welcome in the house of God.

The Clueless

These people don't know the first thing about church. Some of them don't know Jesus from Buddha. If yours is a Pentecostal or Charismatic church, people really don't understand what is going on. If we choose to leave them in the dark, they won't feel welcome and won't come back.

Clueless About Dress. If people have never been to church, they don't know how to dress. We have created an image that portrays people in church dressed in the finest suits and dresses—fine clothes you probably don't have and wouldn't be comfortable wearing if you did. If we are going to survive the tumultuous times ahead, we must summarily dismiss this notion and come to grips with the fact that our world is swiftly changing. Unless we change with it, we will become so outdated and outmoded we will not touch anyone with the life-changing message of Jesus Christ.

Here's a "sacred cow" we need to give up: "When

people go to church, they should dress accordingly." Says who? Certainly not any of the New Testament writers. Why then do we hold to that idea so tenaciously? Maybe from the faulty assumption that says the only time we appear before God is when we enter the doors of a church. We must realize that we are no nearer to God in church than we are when we are working in the yard, grungy clothes and all!

I don't think Jesus cares one bit if you wear the most expensive suit in town or your old beat-up blue jeans. The main reason many of us dress the way we do in church is to impress someone else. Jesus doesn't care!

I am all for modesty and decency, but I have reached the conclusion that even those standards will not stand in the way of Jesus touching someone's life. Neither should they keep us from making someone welcome who isn't properly dressed. If we could follow the example of Jesus and trust Him to work in people's lives, we would all do much better.

Consider the case of a naked man who came to the Lord. He didn't even have on a loin cloth (see Luke 8:27, 35).

Admittedly, if a man walked into the church with no clothes on, we would have him removed. We would try to get him to dress. Our culture and laws and the differences in the setting of that day and this would demand such action. But the essence of the story remains the same. Jesus did not tell the man, "Go and dress up and then I will help you." He helped this man, who later returned clothed and in his right mind (v. 35).

The bottom line is this: Jesus doesn't care what you are wearing and neither should we! If we are going to survive, we must make people feel welcome, regardless of their dress.

Clueless About Our Discussions. People outside the church don't have a clue what we are talking about when we use some of our favorite religious terms. For instance, when I say "regenerated," do you think old Bubba down at the street corner has the slightest idea or concern about what I mean? Of course he doesn't. You can talk to Bubba until you are blue in the face about his need for regeneration and it will do no good whatsoever.

But I tell you what will work. If someone starts to tell Bubba how Jesus died for him and will forgive him of all his sins—he will listen. If someone tells him that through Christ he can have a fresh start in life and the Lord can bring reconciliation in his family—he will understand. If he hears that he is welcome at church and it doesn't matter one bit if all he has to wear is a pair of beat-up pants and scraggly shoes—he will come. The Holy Spirit can take these messages and touch Bubba and change his life forever.

Think of it this way. How many of you enjoy hearing doctors talk their medical jargon in your presence? Is it fun to go to an attorney's office and hear them banter in Latin phrases? I guess the thing I love more than a root canal is hearing computer geeks speaking "computerese" about all the specialized language that characterizes their trade.

While doctors, lawyers, computer whizzes and other secular groups can afford to put you off with their insider discussions, the church cannot. We do not barter in dollars, computer information or even the bodies of men. All those things pass away. We deal in things eternal and cannot afford to build a wall that keeps someone out just because they do not know the secret passwords that allow them entrance into our sacred shrine.

We must strive to speak a language people can understand. It's a tough job. We have been commissioned by Almighty God to take the most wonderful and mysterious secrets of all time and make them available to anyone who desires to know the truth. But He will help us if we will allow Him to transform us first, and then if we welcome everyone no matter their status in life.

Clueless About Our Demonstrations. If those who are raised Catholic venture into a Southern Baptist church, they will be clueless about what happens around them. They won't know when to stand, when to sit, when to sing, or any other participatory gestures. Of course, when those who are raised in a Southern Baptist church drop by a Pentecostal or Charismatic church, they are equally clueless about what is happening. But at least they have some church background.

How do you think someone who hasn't a clue about being a Christian feels when he or she stumbles into a church where people sing, dance, talk in strange tongues, and so on? I tell you how they feel. They want to cry, "Help!" because they are clueless about what is going on.

For that reason, we must work hard to make those who do not understand our particular practices feel welcome. That's hard for some of us to do. But God has called us to make the church a place where everyone can come and encounter His presence. So we must do what it takes.

There are two ways we can help the clueless feel welcome:

1. We can have a solid, Biblical explanation for what happens in church. If we can't defend with Scripture what we do, we probably shouldn't do it!

2. We always want people to know they don't have to act a certain way when they come to a Pentecostal church—they get to! There's a big difference.

We must strive to welcome everyone to our church. They don't have to shout like Brother John or speak in tongues like Sister Sally. But—and this is the great part—they get to shout or speak in tongues if that's how they wish to respond to the moving of the Holy Spirit!

Let's take the pressure off those who don't have a clue and make our church their church. God will bless such an effort with great success and add souls by the score!

The Crushed

In addition to clueless people, there are also "crushed" people. They know all too well how the church works . . . on a carnal basis because they have been hurt. They feel they have been "done in." They have had to endure bad preaching. They have patiently borne up under scathing teaching. They have walked away wounded by conflict. They have suffered the indignity of having their humanness exposed for all to see. In other words, they have walked out of some church wounded, hurt and dazed.

In the Old Testament, the Lord had some rather harsh words for shepherds who mistreated the sheep. In scathing denunciation of their hard practices and uncaring sentiments, God let it be known He was not only calling the shepherds into account, He was also creating places of refuge for struggling sheep. He would touch them with His own hand.

> "Woe to the shepherds who are destroying and scattering the sheep of my pasture!" declares the Lord. Therefore this is what the Lord, the God of Israel, says

to the shepherds who tend my people: "Because you
have scattered my flock and driven them away and have
not bestowed care on them, I will bestow punishment on
you for the evil you have done," declares the Lord. "I
myself will gather the remnant of my flock out of all the
countries where I have driven them and will bring them
back to their pasture, where they will be fruitful and
increase in number" (Jeremiah 23:1-3).

Perhaps you have been injured by men. Perhaps you
have endured the wrath of someone in a church setting
who was given the charge of caring for your soul. Many
of us have walked through a similar experience.

The Lord says He will not only take care of the hard-
hearted shepherd, He will also provide a place of safe
pasture for you. "I will turn Rabbah into a pasture for
camels and Ammon into a resting place for sheep. Then
you will know that I am the Lord" (Ezekiel 25:5).

These were the heathen nations around Israel that had
been instrumental in the judgment of God against the
nation. Yet the Lord was in the process of taking even the
places of wickedness and iniquity and transforming them
into places of safe pasture for the wandering fold.

It gets even better. The Lord says He himself is going
to be involved in searching for the wandering sheep from
His fold.

For this is what the Sovereign Lord says: "I myself will
search for my sheep and look after them. As a shepherd
looks after his scattered flock when he is with them, so

will I look after my sheep. I will rescue them from all the places where they were scattered on a day of clouds and darkness" (34:11, 12).

All those who have been hurt, all those who have been pushed out, all those who feel no one cared for them . . . God is looking for them! We as a church might not be busy looking for them, but our heavenly Father is! We might not think it all that important to become a place where healing can happen, but God thinks we should!

In fact, I am convinced the church the Lord will really use in the last days is the church that says to the hurt and struggling sheep, "You are welcome here!" When the Lord says something akin to what He said through Ezekiel, how can we dare do less?

I myself will tend my sheep and have them lie down, declares the Sovereign Lord. I will search for the lost and bring back the strays. I will bind up the injured and strengthen the weak, but the sleek and the strong I will destroy. I will shepherd the flock with justice (vv. 15, 16).

We must get the message out: "If you are hurting, if you are wounded, if you are weak . . . welcome!"

The Castoffs

Some like to refer to the castoffs of society as the "friends of Jesus." Like it or not, Jesus was equally at ease around the fringes of His society as He was with the wealthy aristocrats of the day. I really think Jesus was more at ease with the castoffs of His day than when He was with the "in" crowd.

One of the things that distinguished Jesus from the other religious teachers of His day was the lunch crowd He ate with. His "lunch bunch" was far beneath the good people of His day, yet those were the very ones Jesus reached out to, and they were also the ones most responsive to His care.

In a passage we usually don't take seriously, Jesus describes a scene from the future. It's a day when all nations are gathered before Him to be judged according to what they have done.

Based on our calloused attitudes we exhibit toward the poor and suffering around us, I give you this warning: *If we take this passage seriously, it will tear us apart and cause us to repent and rush out and do something about the suffering around us.*

> Then the King will say to those on his right, "Come, you who are blessed by my Father; take your inheritance, the kingdom prepared for you since the creation of the world. For I was hungry and you gave me something to eat, I was thirsty and you gave me something to drink, I was a stranger and you invited me in, I needed clothes and you clothed me, I was sick and you looked after me, I was in prison and you came to visit me." Then the righteous will answer

him, "Lord, when did we see you hungry and feed you, or thirsty and give you something to drink? When did we see you a stranger and invite you in, or needing clothes and clothe you? When did we see you sick or in prison and go to visit you?" The King will reply, "I tell you the truth, whatever you did for one of the least of these brothers of mine, you did for me" (Matthew 25:34-40).

Jesus says He is a brother to the hungry guy with a sign begging for food down by the interstate. Jesus claims brotherhood with the stranger who wanders into our church and sits in solitude. Jesus vows He is related to the lady who has tattered clothing to wear to church, and He is a brother to the man dying alone with AIDS. He says He is a close relative of the man locked away for 20 years to life for robbing the liquor store.

That bothers some of us—the fact that Jesus might even look at people like that—not to mention the fact that He might even be their relative. But here's something even more shocking: *He calls on you and me to make these people welcome!* That's what His church is all about.

I know a couple who received a strange invitation for dinner one day. It seems the mother of one of the people in the marriage invited her child over for dinner, but told her the other partner in the marriage wasn't welcome because they were going to discuss the division of the estate after her death. I don't know how you would have responded to that invitation. Personally, I would have made it known that if Diane was not invited, I would not be present under any circumstance. You see, she is part of me. There is no way under the sun you are going to get me to come over for something important like that and say, "You can come, but she isn't welcome." I just won't show up.

How do you think Jesus feels when we tell His family—the hurting, dying, sinful, broken, castoffs of society—"You are not welcome here." I think that's one reason we aren't having revival like we want. We have told the family of Jesus, "Sorry, when you get your act together, you can come inside." I think Jesus is saying back to us, "I'll just stand out here with my brothers while you guys carry on."

I am convinced that revival will sweep the land and the church will spill over with souls when we remove all obstacles and the man with AIDS sits between the alcoholic and the successful businessman with the Armani suit. When the prostitute knows she can come in the church and be welcomed, the Holy Spirit will be poured out like never before.

I believe we are in store for a fiery revival like we have only dreamed of. It will come when we reach the place where the drug addict knows he can walk into our church and we will put our arms around him, pray for him, help him get clean and live free before the Lord. May God create such a place!

That's Risky Business

Is such an undertaking risky? Sure it is. There are a myriad of risks involved. Right up front, there is the risk of offending someone's standards. In most churches, a group of people sociologists call "mall rats" could walk into a church and receive such a glaring stare from the majority of the congregation that they would have to be wearing black asbestos to survive the white-hot gaze. Heaven forbid they hang around and become a part of the youth group. Why? Because parents would start snatching their kids out in a flash. They wouldn't want their children involved with kids like that.

The examples are plentiful. How would most churches respond if a group of 20 prostitutes slipped in and sat on the back pews? (Of course in most churches they would have to sit down front because the faithful, early arrivers claim the back pews. But that's another story.)

Here's one to consider. How would most churches respond if a group of homosexual men started coming in and sitting together because they wanted to find out about God? And what if a bunch of drunkards with the smell of liquor on their breath decided to venture into most churches in America today? How would the church people respond?

The "safe" thing is to respond in the usual way—treat them with such contempt and keep them at such arm's length they never come back. Or, if they are persistent, just be up front and let them know this place is for respectable people.

What if, instead of that common routine, we did something risky and made the "clueless," the "crushed" and the "castoffs" welcome? What would happen? Would they disrupt? Not fit into our routine? Create the occasional disturbance? Yes. But they also might escape hell and enter the kingdom of heaven because we made our church a place of welcome!

The Mind of Christ

What we desperately need is to do what we have said for so long we want to do—become more like Jesus. Paul put it very succinctly: "Let this mind be in you which was also in Christ Jesus" (Philippians 2:5, *NKJV*).

What was the mind of Christ in this matter? Put simply, He welcomed any and all who came to Him. The most incorrigible, the incurable—even the insane—were welcome around Him.

We need to develop the same mind-set the Lord had when He was on earth. We need to renew our minds until our attitudes toward those He wants to reach parallel His own. That's the kind of church He wants us to become. That's the kind of church men and women who are hungry for His presence will want to join. I want to become more like Him. Do you?

In the year that King Uzziah died, I saw the Lord seated on a throne, high and exalted, and the train of his robe filled the temple. Above him were seraphs, each with six wings: With two wings they covered their faces, with two they covered their feet, and with two they were flying. And they were calling to one another: "Holy, holy, holy is the Lord Almighty; the whole earth is full of his glory." At the sound of their voices the doorposts and thresholds shook and the temple was filled with smoke (Isaiah 6:1-4).

3

A Worshiping Church
Part 1

Worship is the central act of any believer's life. The reason we worship is because we are people of God. We are people who know Him. We have discovered His greatness, power and love, and we simply must worship Him. When we really catch a glimpse of Him in His radiant glory—deep, moving, emotional worship will come as naturally as breath.

I am not referring to the flippant "Come on now, somebody raise your hands and praise the Lord" stuff we do and think we have entered into the Holy of Holies. No, this worship of which I speak goes far beyond the fleshly exuberance we love so much. It cuts to the very heart of a man and makes him fall on his face before his Maker in awe, wonder and sometimes fear.

This is the type of worship experienced by Isaiah, the great prophet, when he finally caught a glimpse of the Lord. His story is familiar, but I fear that our familiarity has bred some contempt for the weight the passage lays out for worship in Isaiah 6:1-4.

Isaiah saw the Lord. Most of us think we would like to see the Lord. I don't know about that. I am not so sure we are ready for what would greet us. I think we are stuck in the "flannelgraph" Jesus mode or the modern film versions of Jesus that portray Him as a hippie who just happens, on occasion, to have supernatural power.

Better yet, lots of Americans have swallowed the "dream and vision" Jesus that people claim to have seen. This Jesus is always tender and kind and even violates the written words of the Bible.

A New Level of Worship

The last vision of Jesus I totally trust came from the inspired pen of a fellow named John. John, having spent a number of years with Jesus, had given his life in service to Him. Toward the end of his life, Jesus appeared to John and the old fellow wrote down what the Lord looked like:

> His head and hair were white like wool, as white as snow, and his eyes were like blazing fire. His feet were like bronze glowing in a furnace, and his voice was like

the sound of rushing waters. In his right hand he held seven stars, and out of his mouth came a sharp double-edged sword. His face was like the sun shining in all its brilliance (Revelation 1:14-16).

That's a far cry from the milquetoast Jesus we encounter today, isn't it? But that's the Jesus we are worshiping—One who is awesome, powerful, overcoming, ruling, judging.

I contend that the church needs to experience a new level of worship where we, like Isaiah in the Old Testament, and John in the New Testament, pass beyond the outer court of sacrificial fire and all the "feel-good" stuff, and make our way to the inner sanctum and brush up against God. It will change us, I assure you. It changed Isaiah and John.

In true worship, there's no dancing around, whooping and hollering, high-fiving and backslapping each other. There's no worked-up fervor of excitement that fades the moment we walk out the door on our way to a meal.

What happens when people of God enter this dimension of worship? Observe what Isaiah 6:5 says: "'Woe to me!' I cried. 'I am ruined! For I am a man of unclean lips, and I live among a people of unclean lips, and my eyes have seen the King, the Lord Almighty.'"

Isaiah cried out in repentance. He saw himself in the light of Almighty God and knew he had to take care of some business. John took a different approach. Overwhelmed by the weight of God's glory, he hit the ground like a dead man. "When I saw him, I fell at his feet as though dead. Then he placed his right hand on me and said: 'Do not be afraid. I am the First and the Last' " (Revelation 1:17).

John didn't slump over and slowly sink to the floor. He fell like someone who had been struck dead by a heart attack. John saw this powerful Jesus and decided, "I better get out of His way!" Down he went!

It's time the church moves forward in worship to the place where the glory of God becomes so real, so powerful, we all fall on our faces in His presence. My prayer is for God to show up in church and give us as much of His glory as we can stand, plus a little more. I long for Him to reveal Himself so powerfully that every person in the church does one of two things: falls before Him in worship or flees from Him in fear!

O God, give us a change in our worship! Ironically, worship is one of those sensitive subjects in the church. Trying to move a church toward a new and deeper experience in worship may be the most difficult task a pastor faces today.

To fail to press forward in worship and experience a fresh and new touch of God carries a far greater price than that exacted by some member of the church who is offended. If we fail to follow hard after God, we offend

Him! Please don't get me wrong. I love God's people, but I had rather offend them than offend Him!

Our Modern Bronze Serpent

God's people have this curious and deadly proclivity. We like to establish patterns and set them in concrete. We forget that God is a dynamic and fluid God. On the one hand, God never changes. On the other hand, God is never the same. We forget this and forge God in our image rather than trying to follow Him and find His will in all we do.

Worship is no different. Some of us have made *worship* our God, rather than worshiping God. Here's an interesting tidbit from the Old Testament. A man named Hezekiah ascended to the throne of Judah. He was a king who followed the Lord. He did some interesting house-cleaning upon becoming king:

> He removed the high places, smashed the sacred stones and cut down the Asherah poles. He broke into pieces the bronze snake Moses had made, for up to that time the Israelites had been burning incense to it (It was called Nehushtan.) (2 Kings 18:4).

High places were just that—high elevations where people erected a place of worship. Exactly why those civilizations chose a high elevation to build a place of worship is not known. Some tend to think they viewed the hills as the places where the sky rested, thus the places where the gods settled. What matters is that this king razed all the pagan high places. We are told he also smashed the sacred stones and cut down the Asherah poles. This probably refers to a place where Baal and Asherah were worshiped together. Sacrifices would be made on the stones and sexual immorality carried out beneath the trunk of the Asherah pole (a tree trunk symbolizing life).

Most evangelical, fundamental Christians would rally around that kind of reform. We would probably say, "It's about time somebody stood up for what's right, bless God!" But the verse doesn't end there. Notice what this crazy man of God did next. *He smashed the bronze snake Moses had made!* Is that crazy?

I don't know exactly how many years had passed between Moses making that snake and Hezekiah doing his bull-in-the-china-shop routine. Most scholars estimate more than 700 years, which made that snake on a pole a very valuable piece of art.

Do you have any idea what the value of the *original* Declaration of Independence would be worth? I would say in today's market, you might get a billion dollars for that piece of paper. It's a little over 200 years old. That snake was priceless.

A Place of Worship

Here is what's really interesting and applicable to

every one of us. We may not have billions of dollars to spend on religious artwork, but we tend to do the very thing they did in Judah. Somebody set that pole up in a house of worship and somebody else said, "Hey, let's sing a song and burn some incense in remembrance of what happened." They all did and before you know it, the only proper way to worship was to walk by, drop your money down to purchase some smelly incense, throw it in the fire in front of the pole and go your way.

God said, "I am tired of that junk. I want to send revival. To do so, I must start at the place of worship. Get rid of all that pagan trash. And while you are at it, get rid of all that formula worship that is so tied to a pattern you have forgotten about Me!"

The same thing is happening today. I believe God is showing up in the house of worship and saying, "I am tired of your two songs, take an offering, sing a special, three points, poem, and go home. I am reclaiming the house with My name on it and pouring My glory into it!"

- Our bronze serpent of predictability is being smashed.

- Our bronze serpent of controlling worship so the world won't be offended is being obliterated.

- Our bronze serpent of nice, neatly packaged, always-out-right-on-time services is passing away.

 ○ Our bronze serpent of being able to explain every little detail of what happens in a service is over.

 ○ Our bronze serpent of having to have the singing the way we like it, the music just our style, the entire order of church set to "appeal to our individual tastes or else" is over.

That's right. God has shown up at the gathering place of all our "Stop that sinning, you bunch of wretches" crowds and announced, *"Oh, by the way, I am taking over in here!"*

How will we respond? We can resist what God wants to do. That's right, we can fight against what God wants to do and think we are right all the while. Churches do it every day. Paul told us the last days would be marked by churches that knew all about God, but would not allow His power to be present (see 2 Timothy 3:1-9).

One of the most haunting verses in Scripture is a lament from the heart of God in Hosea 4:17: "Ephraim is joined to idols; leave him alone!"

Sad situation, isn't it? Here were God's people—led by Him, saved by Him, kept by Him—but over the passing of time, turned from serving the living God to worshiping idols. And they were so entrenched in this practice, God was giving up on them!

Similarly, churches by the thousands resist what God wants to do today. They cling with white knuckles to their bronze-serpent patterns of man-dominated worship to the point I believe God says, "Leave them alone! I am through!"

Here's the sad part. Like Samson of old, we don't even know when God left. We carry on, sing our songs, do our stuff, have a good time, and glibly march into a lost and dying world—powerless and ineffective.

We can, however, embrace what the Lord wants to do with us and have His presence flood our lives. We can fling open the doors of our hearts, hand over the reins of our church to Him, and watch with wonder and amazement as He comes in and performs His mighty acts.

Embracing a Move of God

That's the church of Acts 5. Here we find a church that embraced the move of God, even though it was vastly different to anything they had ever seen. It's not often a man clings to his bronze-serpent style of worship that allows him to lie to God, and gets killed for it. Even rarer is when his wife comes in later on in the day with her bronze-serpent worship outline intact and fails to note the entry of her husband's funeral, and she is killed too! That's different!

But the church didn't scatter. They didn't say, "God, stop that! That's bad for business!" Listen to the events following that unexplainable series of occurrences:

Great fear seized the whole church and all who heard about these events. The apostles performed many miraculous signs and wonders among the people. And all the believers used to meet together in Solomon's Colonnade. No one else dared join them, even though they were highly regarded by the people. Nevertheless, more and more men and women believed in the Lord and were added to their number. As a result, people brought the sick into the streets and laid them on beds and mats so that at least Peter's shadow might fall on some of them as he passed by. Crowds gathered also from the towns around Jerusalem, bringing their sick and those tormented by evil spirits, and all of them were healed (Acts 5:11-16).

That church embraced worship. When they embraced a heavy move of God, some of the most astounding things happened.

    ✧ Fear came on them. If we started carrying out those killed by the Lord for their presumption upon His grace, we would probably experience some fear as well. A little fear of God would be good for all of us.

    ✧ Great power flowed out. Signs and wonders happened all over the city.

    ✧ The casual Christian dropped out while the people hungry for God flowed in. If revolving doors were the style in those days, two lines would have formed. The casual Christians, upset over what they perceived as losing their church, would have angrily hit the metal bars and given a great shove as they exited, vowing never to return. The whole time, the door would be swinging anyway, activated by the throngs of hungry men and women trying to get in because they are desperate to meet God.

⌁ Crowds became so desperate for God they started lining the streets so the shadow of Peter might fall over them and bring healing. It wasn't Peter's shadow. It was the shadow of the One with whom Peter was walking that made the difference!

⌁ People from towns all over the countryside started coming just so they could receive a touch from God.

I'll say it again. When a church enters into a place of worship with God—embracing His move—He will do such electrifying things. That's when men clamor over each other to get to where He is. Why do you think people flew to Florida from all over the world to visit the revival in Pensacola? That's why people crowded to Toronto, Canada, and packed a small church in Missouri. That's why in cities all across the world, men and women will cram into hot, stuffy, uncomfortable buildings and put up with all kinds of inconveniences. . . . *the world is looking for a place to meet God!*

Marks of True Worship

Up front, we need to note that styles of worship are not the important issue. All around the world, people gather and worship God in vastly different ways. It isn't style, but substance that matters. Million-dollar pipe organs or cheap guitars mean nothing. The central issue is simple: *How much man can die and how much God can live.* I think we are in line for a lot of funerals if we are going to become Acts 5 churches. These will not be funerals where we go out and bury the dead, although that might have to take place if we aren't willing to die out to self. Rather, we will have some personal funerals where we bury our ambitions, our control, our stubbornness, our bronze serpents of worship, because God *is* going to have a glorious church in the last days and I really don't think He has a problem with taking me out of the way if necessary.

True worship, regardless of the particular style, has some common denominators that cut across every culture, every style. Worship is present in hot, steamy churches in Central and South America, as well as scorching, arid churches in Africa. You will find people in churches worshiping with freezing temperatures and no heat in Siberia, as well as in the most state-of-the-art facility in America.

True Worship Is Real

All pretense is gone. True worship never puts on a

front. It's not a show. It flows from the heart of a man or woman who genuinely loves God more than life. True worship is characterized by those who are so consumed with their love for God that they must express their feelings.

Frankly, I think the majority of our problem stems from a lack of passion for God. We want a "cool" and "acceptable" worship—one that offends no one. But that just won't cut it with God!

We need to learn this: Passionate worship is going to move us deeply, cost us heavily and bring a totally new dimension of God's glory streaming into our lives. I really believe the word from God for the church today is, "Get rid of the lethargy, forget what men have to say and passionately seek My face in worship!" I believe the survival of local churches hinges on just how far they will go in following the stream of God's anointing in worship.

Let's consider the life of David—the most prominent worshiper in the Bible. The man was a worship machine, but could he ever make a mess out of things! In 1 Chronicles 21, David made a major blunder. He sinned by counting the number of men in his army. Not that a census is wrong, but the motive behind the census was the problem.

God's Judgment on David

It's time we understood that God knows both the thoughts and intents of our hearts. David's intent was to

69

know just how big (and bad) he was so he could put just a little less trust in God. God would have none of it and He sent quick and severe judgment on David.

When the census was finished, David thumps his chest and says, "Great! One million, one hundred thousand soldiers. How great I am!" As soon as he signed off on the census, making it a part of public and official record, a knock was heard on the palace door. Someone told David that Gad, the prophet, was outside. He comes in and confirms what David had already realized. . . . *David blew it!*

Now, here's one for all those of us who think God is so predictable in everything He does. God gives David a choice. He can select curtain one, two or three.

⌂ Curtain 1—three years of famine.

⌂ Curtain 2—three months of battle loss to his enemy.

⌂ Curtain 3—three days of plague from God.

Not exactly what those on game shows hope to find waiting as their grand prize, but that's what David was given. Here's what bothers me about the whole thing . . . they are paying for David's pride! Seventy thousand men. And if you study it closely, you come to the conclusion that 70,000 soldiers fell dead to a plague because David got the bighead.

Before you start pointing a finger at God and shouting about how unfair He is, remember this: Every year, millions of men and women die only to spend eternity in hell, all because the church of the living God refuses to fall to her face and do whatever it takes to have the precious oil of God's anointed presence!

It's time we find the real worship of David at the threshing floor. People's eternal destinies hinge on what we do.

David suffers a great loss—70,000 men. Roughly one of every 13 of his soldiers fell dead. The slaughter was so great, so horrific, God himself finally said to the angel of death, "Enough!" David grasps at what happened and said, "It's time to worship." God's Word vividly describes what happened next:

> Then the angel of the Lord ordered Gad to tell David to go up and build an altar to the Lord on the threshing floor of Araunah the Jebusite. So David went up in obedience to the word that Gad had spoken in the name of the Lord. While Araunah was threshing wheat, he turned and saw the angel; his four sons who were with him hid themselves. Then David approached, and when Araunah looked and saw him, he left the threshing floor and bowed down before David with his face to the ground. David said to him, "Let me have the site of your threshing floor so I can build an altar to the Lord, that the plague on the people may be stopped. Sell it to me at the full price." Araunah said to David, "Take it! Let my lord the king do whatever pleases him. Look, I will give the oxen for the burnt offerings, the threshing sledges for the wood, and the wheat for the grain offering. I will give all

this." But King David replied to Araunah, "No, I insist on paying the full price. I will not take for the Lord what is yours, or sacrifice a burnt offering that costs me nothing." So David paid Araunah six hundred shekels of gold for the site. David built an altar to the Lord there and sacrificed burnt offerings and fellowship offerings. He called on the Lord, and the Lord answered him with fire from heaven on the altar of burnt offering (1 Chronicles 21:18-26).

There was no way David was going to try and get by on someone else's worship. Realizing he had to touch God for himself, David dug deep. He bought the land from the owner. In the process, David gave him about 15 pounds of gold. I checked the price of gold on the Internet (1/27/03) and found that gold was selling for $370.10 an ounce. At today's prices, David bought that hard spot on the ground for about $88,824.

Costly? Sure was. Worth it? You better believe it. Look what happened when David entered this new dimension of worship. I have read about David, preached about David, but until this point, I had missed this part of his life. David worshiped and God sent fire from heaven to consume the offering (v. 26)!

Moses had seen it. Gideon had seen it (Judges 6:21). Elijah would see it. David wasn't going to have to spend the rest of his life talking about those who had seen the fire or prophesying about those who would see the fire. He experienced the fire for himself. No longer did he have to hear about a move of God and wish he could have one like they were having. His worship brought his personal encounter with God. That's what real worship will do. It will cut deeply into your whole life and bring you face-to-face with the grandeur of the Almighty.

Ascribe to the Lord the glory due his name;
worship the Lord in the splendor of his holiness
(Psalm 29:2).

4 A Worshiping Church
Part 2

I want to do more than hear about a great move of God. I want to do more than listen to prophecies about a future move of God. I want to somehow find that place where He is moving and go there so I can be changed by His presence.

Once we find it, we won't leave the same! We may leave with singed hair from the fire like David, or we may have a halting limp like Jacob, a burned face like Moses at the bush, a new tongue like the people in the Upper Room, or an anointed glow like the disciples after they had been with Jesus. That leads to another common denominator of true worship.

True Worship is Regenerative

Not that worship saves, or regenerates us in the theological sense of having sins forgiven, but true worship changes us. We simply cannot enter the presence of a holy God and remain unchanged. These are tough words, but they must be heeded if we are going to be what God wants us to be. People are tired of watching the same people who shouted, danced, hooted and hollered and talked in tongues waltz out of church and be the same mean-spirited people with sour dispositions who gossip and sow discord.

We don't want to admit it, but we can come to church, do a little shouting, a little speaking in tongues, jerk around some and leave smiling—proclaiming to everyone how great church was. Within hours they see us stab our brother in the back or act like we have never heard of Jesus. It happens all the time and that's one reason the world passes us by. They have watched us, heard us, seen how we act when it is all over and concluded it's all a sham. Sadly, quite often they are correct!

Let me give you a case in point. At a large camp meeting, I watched a man respond to an altar call. The service was full of shouting. Spiritually, it was about a mile wide and an inch deep. The evangelist called for anyone who wanted a touch from God to come to the altar. Suddenly, a man I knew personally who was a two-faced, hypocritical, tale-bearing, discord-sowing individual ran to the altar. He shook, jerked, fell to the floor and rolled around. I stood unmoved.

You can say, "Pastor, you were judging that man." Perhaps I was. But that's the point I am trying to make. For years this man exhibited all the signs of "Pentecostal praise" while acting like the devil's nephew in church. It has always been the same. Consequently, he can tap-dance on a balcony railing and I will pass it off as nothing more than a show. He has never been changed by his encounter with God.

The world points to the church and says, "What you have is no different than the booze I drink, the drugs I take, the sexual escapades I encounter. You are just like we are—you have a good time and when it's over, you are exactly the same person you were going in." It rips me apart to admit it, but they are right!

In the Bible, men who went beyond the fleshly stimulating pattern of praise (where everyone leaves with a smile and a promise to come back next week), and pressed into real worship so far they began to sense some of the glory of God, were changed!

Take Moses, for instance. By the time you read about him in Exodus 34, he has been with the Lord for some time. He has heard the voice of God. He has witnessed a portion of the glory of God. Take a look at him as he lumbers down the rocky hillside, staggering back to the camp.

> When Moses came down from Mount Sinai with the two tablets of the Testimony in his hands, he was not aware that his face was radiant because he had spoken with the Lord. When Aaron and all the Israelites saw Moses, his face was radiant, and they were afraid to come near him. But Moses called to them; so Aaron and all the leaders of the community came back to him, and he spoke to them. Afterward all the Israelites came near

77

him, and he gave them all the commands the Lord had given him on Mount Sinai. When Moses finished speaking to them, he put a veil over his face. But whenever he entered the Lord's presence to speak with him, he removed the veil until he came out. And when he came out and told the Israelites what he had been commanded, they saw that his face was radiant. Then Moses would put the veil back over his face until he went in to speak with the Lord (vv. 29-35).

He came back from that encounter with God glowing like a radioactive isotope. Not many knew what had happened, but everyone knew something had happened. They saw a marked change in the man.

In verse 8 we are told why he was different: "Moses bowed to the ground at once and worshiped."

He was on his face before God. He found more than "Holy Ghost goose bumps" or "the power to shout" on that rocky hillside. He found the glory of God, and it changed his life forever.

In typical fashion, the religious establishment said, "Moses, we can't have this. We can't take this. Put on a veil until you calm down. Mask it over until it subsides." Moses said, "Fine, I'll do my best to help you, but this isn't going to stop as easily as you think. I am going back!"

If we press on—if we keep crying, "More, Lord; take me out deeper"—there will be those around us who won't like it. They will make fun of us and get upset with us. May God birth in us a desire so deep for Him that we actually come to the place where we no longer care what others say!

Here's why the church—my church, your church—must press on in and have a regenerative experience in God: "But whenever he entered the Lord's presence to speak with him, he removed the veil until he came out. And when he came out and told the Israelites what he had been commanded . . . " (vv. 34, 35).

The only hope for this lost world is God. The church is the messenger of God, but the world won't listen to us until we are changed! However, when we have a fresh encounter with God—glowing like Moses, empowered like the 120—the world will stop and take notice once more.

This was what happened in Acts 2. Pentecostals love this passage and we should. After all, the 120 trudged up the stairs, but they tumbled down them. The whole city of Jerusalem noticed a difference in them after a regenerating worship encounter with God. O God, give us this!

Notice the setup in this encounter. Luke gives us a snapshot of their activity:

> When he had led them out to the vicinity of Bethany, he lifted up his hands and blessed them. While he was blessing them, he left them and was taken up into heaven. Then they worshiped him and returned to Jerusalem with great joy. And they stayed continually at the temple, praising God (Luke 24:50-53).

Here is where most Pentecostals and Charismatics now dwell. It's fun. We like it. Lots of good things happen here. We come to church and have a good time. Occasionally, God will visit us with a touch of His presence and some

79

wonderful things take place. A few people will get healed. Someone will get saved. Someone talks in another tongue. Joy erupts. Some folks might shout, dance, wave their hands or a banner. All in all, we leave feeling pretty good about ourselves.

What we have not grasped is the inherent danger of staying right there. In the first-century church, 500 people started, but only 120 remained faithful. That means 380 people quit! In 10 days, their church dropped from 500 to just over 100. In virtually any church-governing system, someone would be in trouble. If that happened today, the pastor would be packing. Of course, it had nothing to do with the pastor. I guess you could say the apostle Peter was the lead guy. At least he was on the Day of Pentecost, so he probably had a leading role through the whole ordeal.

Can't you see the meeting now? About seven or eight of the original bunch meet and say, "You know, we gotta do something here! We are dying like crazy. Perhaps it's time for a leadership change." Then they started talking about what was going on.

△ We can't fault the worship because people are really having a good time.

△ There's not a griping and grumbling problem, everyone seems to be experiencing joy.

△ You can't point a finger at the meeting times, we are continually in church.

⚑ Yet, our number has fallen from around 500 to around 100. What's the problem?

The problem then is the same one we face today. If all we are ever going to do is come together, have a good time, shout a little, run to God with our "want" lists, go through some motions that release religious tension, we are going to struggle to maintain where we are. As a matter of fact, we will lose ground to the better show across town.

But, when we decide to really get serious about worship and come into the presence of God as never before and allow Him to place His hand on our lives, our churches will make a 180-degree turn. People will flock to be near the presence of the Lord.

It happened to the church in the Book of Acts. They had fallen off to 120. But in one short afternoon, they grew to 3,120! That, my friend, is church growth!

What happened? They had a regenerative worship experience. They went into that Upper Room one way, met more of God than they had ever encountered, and came out totally different.

Worship any way you want—shout, dance, cry, kneel, lay on your face, sit still and be silent. The method is not the point. Just get into His presence and let Him lean heavily upon you until you are changed. Stay there until He has spoken to you. Don't rush out like you have something more important to do. Linger before Him until His conviction comes. Tarry before Him until His consolation is yours. Remain in His presence until a new fire ignites in your heart. Anchor yourself in His presence until He has placed within you a hunger for His holiness like never before.

God is looking for a church that will seek Him in just such a manner so that He might pour out His glory upon it. The world is looking for just such a church where they can encounter the Divine One. I want to be part of just such a church. How about you?

Worship Is Relational

One last thought about true worship—*it's relational.* True worship, while real and regenerative, goes beyond just making you feel better. It changes you so radically that you must share what God has done with the people who desperately need to know Christ.

Far too often, we have received a touch from God that made us feel better, but we never made one dent into the darkness that surrounded us. I believe we decided to cloister ourselves into tight-knit groups of like-minded believers. To our shame, we erected walls, excluding those with even the slightest bit of doctrinal difference— not to mention the lost world around us.

True worship—the kind where you meet God—not only breaks you open, it also spills you out before the world so they can see the Lord. With only a minimal understanding of the events of Acts 2, you grasp this salient fact: *God meant for them to relate to the people in that city who needed Jesus.*

It's no different for us today. God wants to meet us, change us, crush us until nothing is left but His fragrance. Then He wants to send us out into a lost world so they can smell Him emanating from our very being. Only then will others decide they want what we have.

A church pursuing God through worship, but desiring men to come and feel welcome, hinges on this conundrum: *If we get too carried away in worship, people will think we are strange and won't come back.* That is a puzzle I do not have the ability to put together. Trying to please God and trying to make a church acceptable to the palates of men is like trying to piece together a totally blank puzzle with millions of pieces in a dark room while being blindfolded and wearing thick leather gloves. In other words, I guess it can be done, but good luck trying to pull it off!

This whole issue of really pursuing God and worrying about people's reactions and opinions has been a struggle for me. I have heard people say (usually unaware of my church affiliation), "I went to one of those churches where people stood up, shouted, danced and talked in strange tongues. I won't ever go back!"

I have endured the bitter pain of having some of my best friends drift away from church and tell me they had asked their young children, "Would you invite your friends to this church?" They allowed 9-year-old kids to make the choice to leave a church because they did not like the actions of some people who were really pursuing God. I have grimaced and squirmed, wondering about my own sense of direction when I have heard denominational leaders in Pentecostal churches talk about how they have put their hands on the worship services in order to tone them down so visitors wouldn't think they were a cult.

For years I struggled with the whole issue of Pentecostal or Charismatic worship. Finally, I reached a conclusion that although it may be Biblical, it doesn't settle well when you lay it beside church-growth manuals. After all, the central theme of this whole exercise hinges on the statement, "If I could find that church, I'd join it."

Having said that, I think it is time we settled this issue once and for all: *The primary purpose of the church is to lift Him up, not draw in the world.* The primary purpose of the church is not some evangelism program, not teaching Sunday school, not building new facilities, not knocking on every door in town, not feeding hungry people. The primary purpose of the church is to exalt Jesus Christ.

Here's the catch. When we lift Him up in the church, He will speak clearly to His people who will do evangelism, knock on doors, drive buses, teach Sunday school and feed hungry people. The really wonderful part is they won't have to be cajoled or put on a guilt trip to do those works when Jesus speaks. They will do what He says with or without someone recruiting them.

Much of what we do in church today is designed to make us comfortable without the slightest consideration of what makes God comfortable. The church world spends billions of dollars every year making sure everyone is comfortable. For example, consider how we seat people in church. In the first-century church, they met mostly in homes. That meant you sat on whatever furnishings the home provided. When the crowd grew, people sat on the floor. One guy sat in a window one night when Paul was preaching. As preachers often do, Paul got a little long in his exposition and the poor guy fell asleep and fell out of the window. Only the power of God, through the apostle, prevented them from having a funeral that week (see Acts 20:9-12).

Later, it was decided that wooden benches would be better. So, rough-hewn lumber was nailed together for people to sit on. It was a step above the floor, but not much to speak of.

Next came church pews. Not only seats, but backs! No doubt boring preaching contributed greatly to this addition. It is difficult to fall asleep when you have no back support! Pews evolved as we discovered they could be slanted and curved to help support the back.

The Comfortable Church

Then—and for this many are extremely grateful to God—someone came up with the idea of putting padding on the pews. Suddenly, you could not only sit with comfort, you could actually sleep! Today, modular church furniture has arrived. Chairs that offer great lumbar support, deep comfort and great flexibility are the norm.

Think of it. After hundreds of years of research and testing, millions of dollars are spent so we can be comfortable for a couple of hours on Sunday and whatever time we spend during the week. Am I denouncing that effort? No! Am I in favor of going back to sitting on the floor? Not on your life! I thank God for modern conveniences. I love worshiping in an air-conditioned building. I like going to church on a cold winter day and praising the Lord in a warm building. I thank God for modern sound systems and projection systems. Computer-generated graphics and digitally mastered recordings are tremendous.

But, in all our efforts to make men comfortable and appeal to their senses, is it possible we have forgotten what makes us comfortable and what makes God comfortable can be totally different? Is it possible that we have reversed the order of things by making people the honored guests of God rather than placing Him at the very center of all we do?

I am afraid our Americanized model of church has become so self-centered that God is often relegated to the shadows. Don't misunderstand me. I want people to flock to the house of God, so I pray for a packed house. But, what good is accomplished if all they encounter when they come to church is a neatly packaged sermon from preachers who spout religious platitudes and are exuberant but are never changed by God's power?

If God isn't present to change lives, the most crowded church facility in America conducting 10 services each Sunday is nothing more than a religious gathering. Harsh words? Perhaps. But it's time we come to grips with this sobering fact: *We—especially the churches in America—are in a struggle for our very lives.* We must stop looking at the few bright spots in this country when it comes to great churches, thinking we are really making a great difference, and realize this nation is speeding recklessly into a dark spiritual oblivion. All our "stuff" isn't going to turn it around. Only a divine visitation from God will save us. *It's time we find out what makes God feel at home and throw out the welcome mat for Him!*

What Does God Like?

What if we decided to throw caution to the wind and pose that question directly to God? Most likely His answer would be: "I have already told you how I like things!" After all, that's what David discovered when he tried to bring the ark of the covenant back into Jerusalem. David knew something so many of us have missed—the presence of God and how His glory will produce more for the Kingdom in an hour than our efforts can accomplish in a lifetime.

David knew that, but he had to learn a hard lesson. David thought he could simply do as he wished. Without asking God what He thought about things, David ordered the ark brought into the city.

> They moved the ark of God from Abinadab's house on a new cart, with Uzzah and Ahio guiding it. David and all the Israelites were celebrating with all their might before God, with songs and with harps, lyres, tambourines, cymbals and trumpets (1 Chronicles 13:7, 8).

It was a great time. They had church. But no one stopped to ask God, "What do *You* want done here?" As a result, a terrible price was paid.

> The Lord's anger burned against Uzzah, and he struck him down because he had put his hand on the ark. So he died there before God. Then David was angry because the Lord's wrath had broken out against Uzzah, and to this day that place is called Perez Uzzah (vv. 10, 11).

Poor Uzzah gave his life because David did not take time to hear from God. When you look at the literal meaning of the word *perez*, it brings to mind a gruesome sight. It means God sent some force of power into the man that struck him down like a bolt of lightning. No wonder David was afraid!

What did David do? Unlike us, he did not crawl off in a corner and sulk, saying things like, "Well, if that's the way things are going to be, I just won't go back to church!"

What are you going to do when God kills your favorite form of worship? How is the church going to deal with the pressure when no one—including God—is remotely interested in the form of worship we have created? We better devise an answer quickly. God is not the slightest bit interested in our forms of religion. And the world has turned its back on us as well. We must find out how to please somebody, and I have decided I want to please God. I want God to feel at home in my church!

David went back to the Word of God and discovered that the ark was never intended to be carried on a cart. God had set a pattern and declared His way best. When they found that pattern and went back to what God had said, the Lord poured out His glory in the city. When the church returns to the pattern established by the Lord himself, He will come in glory once more and sweep us up in the power of His might.

Where can we find God? How can we come into the presence of the Lord? These questions are answered in Psalm 22:3: "But thou art holy, O thou that inhabitest the praises of Israel" (KJV).

God's Word tells us He will inhabit our praises. That's interesting, because the Lord had already told Israel where He would meet with them: "There, above the cover between the two cherubim that are over the ark of the Testimony, I will meet with you and give you all my commands for the Israelites" (Exodus 25:22).

God would manifest His presence above the mercy seat between the two angels who spread their wings over the ark. We have a prophetic type of worship in the angels. It speaks to the church today, but we must be willing to listen. It gives us the clear picture of what kind of praise makes God feel at home. All we have to do is note how the angels were made and follow the pattern.

> And make two cherubim out of hammered gold at the ends of the cover. Make one cherub on one end and the second cherub on the other; make the cherubim of one piece with the cover, at the two ends. The cherubim are to have their wings spread upward, overshadowing the cover with them. The cherubim are to face each other, looking toward the cover (Exodus 25:18-20).

Right between the tips of the angels' wings was the precise place where the glory of the Lord would meet them. When our praise mirrors those angels, God will meet with us as well. It is interesting to find that the term *cherubim* closely resembles an Akkadian term meaning "to bless, praise or adore." God is showing us clearly that our praise will be the place where He demonstrates His presence.

Three qualities of those angels must be present in our worship.

1. *First, the angels were boiled.* That gold had been through the purifying process, which removes the impurities and leaves nothing but the pure mineral. Fire had been applied to the point that the cauldron had gotten so hot nothing was left but the pure gold.

That can be a painful process. If the gold could speak, it would cry out something like, "Why are you doing this to me?" It can't understand the process any more than we can understand our lives when God places us in the crucible and turns on the heat. We cry out, "O God, get me out of here!" Meanwhile, our Father tells us, "Just wait. When things are finished in your life, you will be pure gold—something I can use." This comes back to the premise: *There will only be more of God in our lives when there is less of us.* By going through the fire, we can become vessels of honor, fit for His use.

2. *The angels were beaten.* They were not made of a mold, but they were beaten by a hammer into the shape God desired. If God had wanted them exactly alike, He would have had the people make a mold and pour the boiling gold into it. God does not expect each of us to be exactly alike in our worship. Just as the hammer would beat a pattern into the gold that differed slightly, so life touches each of us in different ways. Thus, our responses to God will vary.

Some have never been deeply touched by pain. They might not bear the scars of life and respond to the Lord just like someone who has been through the valley and back. That's OK. Their worship may take on a different tone. But if they have been through the fire of God and come out pure in His sight, He knows and accepts their praise.

That's why when we really come to a place where God

shows up, many different responses appear. Some fall to the floor, some cry, some laugh, some dance, some shout, some simply lift their hands in silence. It's time the church understands that no two cherubim were exactly alike, but the hammer marks reflected the glory of God. So, whatever is your life's story, let it bring glory to God.

3. *The angels were bowed.* Both were bowing, wings almost touching each other. They had submitted to the glory of the One who occupied the space above the mercy seat.

Right here is where so many of us miss our opportunity to really know God. We are going to endure the boiling and the beating when life turns up the heat and pounds us with pressure. We can't escape that. Being a good Christian doesn't exempt anyone. It might even make things worse! No, the only difference is when we bow before the Lord and submit to His plan.

Let's see this in action. We find one incident in the New Testament when two of God's choice servants discovered the place between the cherubim, but it cost them to get there.

> They brought them before the magistrates and said, "These men are Jews, and are throwing our city into an uproar by advocating customs unlawful for us Romans to accept or practice." The crowd joined in the attack against Paul and Silas, and the magistrates ordered them to be stripped and beaten. After they had been severely flogged, they were thrown into prison, and the jailer was commanded to guard them carefully. Upon receiving such

orders, he put them in the inner cell and fastened their feet in the stocks. About midnight Paul and Silas were praying and singing hymns to God, and the other prisoners were listening to them. Suddenly there was such a violent earthquake that the foundations of the prison were shaken. At once all the prison doors flew open, and everybody's chains came loose (Acts 16:20-26).

After the boiling hatred of the religious world had burned them and the beating pressure of the whips had lashed them, how would they respond? I know how I would probably respond. I would be just like some of you.

⌁ If that's how God is going to treat me, forget Him!

⌁ If that's what being a Christian is all about, count me out!

⌁ If that's how things are going to be, I am going back!

Not Paul and Silas. They had learned the importance of bowing after the boiling and beating. It brought the glory of God into their lives. The glory brought freedom and salvation for many around them.

Let God boil impure attitudes about worship out of us. Let God beat out our inflexibility and stiffness in worship. Let's bow and submit our lives to Him, crying after Him like a starving child begging for bread. We will see Him as never before and He will be the fire that draws men to His church.

For though we live in the world, we do not wage war as the world does. The weapons we fight with are not the weapons of the world. On the contrary, they have divine power to demolish strongholds. We demolish arguments and every pretension that sets itself up against the knowledge of God, and we take captive every thought to make it obedient to Christ (2 Corinthians 10:3-5).

A Warring Church

If I could find a church at war, I'd love to join it. I think it is a powerful thing to be part of the last-day church that goes to war with the Enemy of our soul. Unfortunately, many church members have concluded the same thing as Paul: we are at war. However, they have directed their salvos at the wrong side of the battle. Rather than taking on the Enemy of men's souls, they have taken on the men. This not only hurts the people in the battle, but it also makes us so ugly, so undesirable, no one wants to have anything to do with us.

We are in a war—but not with each other. Paul made it clear to the Ephesian church just who the Enemy is: "For our struggle is not against flesh and blood, but against the rulers, against the authorities, against the powers of this dark world and against the spiritual forces of evil in the heavenly realms" (6:12).

It's really sad, but over the years far too many of our brothers and sisters have fallen prey to what the military terms "friendly fire." This happens when someone drops a bomb or lobs a shell and kills his own comrades. He doesn't know it, but his action caused their deaths. He may later be sorry for what he did, but that doesn't bring back the victims.

In God's kingdom, we are never at war with each other. We may have our differences, but we are on the same team and our common Enemy is the devil. He is the one with whom we war.

Everyone Fights at Some Time

You might not be in a pitched battle at the moment, but someone is. And they desperately need to find someone who will join them in the fight. The church is having a rough time because we are fighting battles that are not relevant.

⬧ Do you really think the world is the slightest bit interested in the name of a church? No, but we will fight tooth and nail over what it is called.

⬧ Do you think lost men and women really care one iota whether you sing a song from a book or from a screen? So why do we fight over such trivial matters?

⬧ Can't you just picture a couple getting up on Sunday morning. He is reading the paper while smoking a cigar; she's in the kitchen making breakfast. They scan the paper and he says, "Hey honey, let's forget about going to the lake today. The First Church is offering a sermon series on the premillennial, pre-Rapture positions of historical Christianity."

The world does not care about some of the battles we fight and are willing to take a life-and-death stand on. The world is so messed up, so hurt, so wounded; all it wants to know is whether or not anyone in the church can make a difference.

Many people are like a man who got off an airplane one day. The landing had been horrible. The pilot came in at too high a speed, hit the runway with a neck-jarring thud and screeched to a halt just before crashing into the terminal. It was the policy of the airline for the pilot to greet everyone disembarking. His landing had been so shoddy he could barely look them in the eyes. Luckily, no one said much until one fellow looked at the pilot and said, "Hey, did we land or were we shot down?"

It seems like that's what is going on in the world with rough landings:

⌂ Unexpected bills put pressure on the finances.

⌂ Layoffs blow up in your face.

⌂ Kids bring home bad grades.

⌂ The spot in the X-ray is treatable.

Then occasionally we have crash landings:

⌂ Kids wind up on drugs.

⌂ The spot is inoperable cancer.

People are looking for someone to fight with them in the trenches. No one can do that like the church. No one can stand against the foes of our society like the church. I believe nothing causes Satan more sleepless nights than a church with spiritual resources, standing toe-to-toe against all he has to offer. He knows a church like that is unstoppable.

Where Is Your Goliath?

The picture you get from the hours prior to David's great victory over Goliath is hilarious but sad. And not a bad portrait of the church today. Let's take a moment to analyze the whole story recorded in 1 Samuel 17. I want to focus on just a few highlights.

First, there was a lot of parading, but little fighting going on.

> Early in the morning David left the flock with a shepherd, loaded up and set out, as Jesse had directed. He reached the camp as the army was going out to its battle positions, shouting the war cry. Israel and the Philistines were drawing up their lines facing each other (vv. 20, 21).

For 40 days, they lined up, looked each other in the eye and shouted the battle cry at each other. They looked good, sounded good, dressed good—but no one was fighting! I especially love what Eliab said when David came into camp.

> When Eliab, David's oldest brother, heard him speaking with the men, he burned with anger at him and asked, "Why have you come down here? And with whom did you leave those few sheep in the desert? I know how conceited you are and how wicked your heart is; you came down only to watch the battle" (v. 28).

If I had been David, I couldn't have resisted the temptation to say, "Battle? What battle?" There was a lot of talking going on, but there was no fighting.

The second thing I notice about this whole episode is the real reason there was no fighting. It was *Goliath!* He was the World Heavyweight Boxing Champ, World's Strongest Man, Navy Seal, Army Ranger, Marine Sniper, martial arts champion—all rolled into one! He was the biggest, baddest, toughest, meanest, most dangerous thing walking the planet at the time!

> A champion named Goliath, who was from Gath, came out of the Philistine camp. He was over nine feet tall. He had a bronze helmet on his head and wore a coat of scale armor of bronze weighing five thousand shekels; on his legs he wore bronze greaves, and a bronze javelin was slung on his back. His spear shaft was like a weaver's rod, and its iron point weighed six hundred shekels. His shield bearer went ahead of him (vv. 4-7).

Today we have diminished this giant's stature by retelling the story. Goliath was a murderous arm of wrath protruding from the Philistine army. He was a terror who had no mercy. When he told David he intended to feed him to the birds, he literally meant he was going to dismember him and scatter him over a field so the scavenging birds would feast on his grisly remains.

No wonder there was no fighting. Faced with such an enemy, most of us would also slink back into camp. What's really interesting is the fact that there are many Goliaths running around today. No, you won't find any 9-foot-tall giants with body armor and .50-caliber machine guns standing on the hillsides screaming out epithets against the people of God. But there are still Goliaths galore.

- *Millions are facing a Goliath of financial pressure.* Crushing heaviness occupies every waking moment, wondering how they are going to make it.

- *Millions are facing a Goliath of addiction.* Drugs, alcohol, food, sex and gambling have driven them to the edge of despair and insanity.

- *Millions are facing a Goliath of loneliness.* Living virtually alone in a crowded world, they feel isolated and insulated from any loving human contact.

- *Countless others face a Goliath of fear.* Fears of failure, rejection and cancer gnaw at them daily.

And what about that Goliath of guilt? Guilt shouts at us about what worthless subjects we are to the King of kings.

Millions have given up the fight and surrendered to an attitude of "Whatever will be will be; there's nothing I can do about it." They have surrendered to a gaudy Goliath because they are afraid to fight.

Let's take one last look at this intriguing picture. When someone takes on the giant, others will run to join in the fight. That's right, when someone—the church or a ministry—stands up to Goliath and knocks him down, people flock to that place and rejoice because they have wanted to see him defeated for a long time!

While everyone else was standing around in fear, saying, "He's just too big to fight," David grabbed a handful of stones and said, "He's just too big to miss." The aim was true and the rock did its work. The giant went down and David used the giant's own sword to finish him off. What happened next is seldom mentioned: "Then the men of Israel and Judah surged forward with a shout and pursued the Philistines to the entrance of Gath and to the gates of Ekron. Their dead were strewn along the Shaaraim road to Gath and Ekron" (v. 52).

Men came out of hiding and joined David. They ran to where the giant killer was and pressed on. Why? Because someone had taken on their giant and brought deliverance into their lives.

When men know the church is going to join them in the battle for their freedom, they will come to the house of God. For so long we have been the enemy. We haven't been warring to set them free. The only wars some churches ever have are those over who gets to play the piano or what color the carpet is going to be. Those who are enslaved by a Goliath of alcoholism or homosexuality can just forget about coming to most churches for help. All they will receive is further entrenchment in the guilt trench.

Don't you think it is time for the church of the living God to turn away from our lists of reasons why we should fight each other and instead fight Goliath? After all, David had every right to say things like . . .

♦ Why don't you guys get up and fight?

♦ Get a job and go to work against the enemy.

♦ If you would help yourself, the Lord would help you.

♦ If you are so afraid, how can you possibly call yourself a soldier of God?

For years the church has ambled into the camp of those facing a dreaded Goliath of their own and said hurtful things like . . .

♦ Get a job and take care of your own.

♦ You can get out of that addiction if you really try.

♦ Clean up your act and then you can join us.

⌂ We don't want your kind around here, so go somewhere else.

They are suffering and dying because they don't have the power to slay the giant in their lives. They thought we might have that power, but if we do, we don't share it.

When a church decides to link up with the hurting and go to war against the spiritual Goliaths of the day, men will come because they want to be set free.

The All-Time, Undisputed Champion

Many comparisons can be drawn from the day when David killed Goliath. Most paint the church as the army of Israel, hiding in the trenches because of Goliath. Perhaps that's a good analogy. There's one thing we really don't have, however. When you cast David as champion, he does not compare to the real Champion—the Champion of Calvary. Jesus outshines David like an erupting volcano outshines a nightlight in a child's bedroom. There is none to compare.

The reason why the church can take on any spiritual Goliath roaming the earth today is because *Jesus Christ, the hope of glory is with us!*

It's easy to get carried away and overly excited when you consider just how powerful our Jesus really is. One story from His life illustrates His immense power over every Goliath you and I face:

They sailed to the region of the Gerasenes, which is across the lake from Galilee. When Jesus stepped ashore, he was met by a demon-possessed man from the town. For a long time this man had not worn clothes or lived in a house, but had lived in the tombs. When he saw Jesus, he cried out and fell at his feet, shouting at the top of his voice, "What do you want with me, Jesus, Son of the Most High God? I beg you, don't torture me!" For Jesus had commanded the evil spirit to come out of the man. Many times it had seized him, and though he was chained hand and foot and kept under guard, he had broken his chains and had been driven by the demon into solitary places. Jesus asked him, "What is your name?" "Legion," he replied, because many demons had gone into him. And they begged him repeatedly not to order them to go into the Abyss. A large herd of pigs was feeding there on the hillside. The demons begged Jesus to let them go into them, and he gave them permission. When the demons came out of the man, they went into the pigs, and the herd rushed down the steep bank into the lake and was drowned (Luke 8:26-33).

Verse 27 is a powerful word picture. We read where Jesus was "met" by a man full of demons. That word is interesting. It is a compound word in the Greek language consisting of two words that mean "to oppose and to be under." The man who opposed Jesus was full of demons, but they were subject to His mighty power.

I believe the moment the front of His sandaled foot touched the dirt of the shores of Gadara, an alarm sounded throughout the spiritual forces in that whole region,

"He's here!" The thousands of demons tormenting that poor man shuddered in terror, "He's here!"

There is a powerful principle of spiritual warfare before us. You may think you have to know the names of demons, know their powers and understand how they work. I believe if we can just get Jesus to show up, it won't matter about who the demon is or what his place is in the hierarchy. It is simply no contest when Jesus shows up!

Pay close attention to this encounter. Note the posture of the demons recorded by Luke in verse 28: "When he saw Jesus, he cried out and fell at his feet, shouting at the top of his voice, 'What do you want with me, Jesus, Son of the Most High God? I beg you, don't torture me!'"

The demons are on the ground begging Jesus, "Don't torture us!" What a contrast. When demons deal with men, they rule with vicious nastiness. They are cruel and merciless. Look at how they treated the poor man:

For Jesus had commanded the evil spirit to come out of the man. Many times it had seized him, and though he was chained hand and foot and kept under guard, he had broken his chains and had been driven by the demon into solitary places (Luke 8:29).

That's why I can't stand the devil! If I were God, I would take Satan by his bulbous head and squeeze it like a grape until it popped and tell all the demons looking on, "This is what I will do to any of you who even look a second time at my children!" I look forward to the day when Satan is chained and thrown into the pit forever!

When Jesus shows up, demons flee because they are no match for the King of kings. He has a personal plan for them and they know what is going to take place in the future. They cannot stand to be around where He is manifested as King of kings and Lord of lords.

That's why the church must have the presence of the Lord in its midst. That's why the church must go to war with the Enemy of men's souls in total surrender to the Head of the church, Jesus Christ.

The Safest Place to Do Battle

In every battle, there are places that are safer than others. If you are in a deep foxhole, you are much safer than if you are standing in the line of fire. If you are concealed in the bushes, you are much safer than if you are standing out in the open. In every battle, you and I need a covering. We have it!

Joshua discovered it when he was preparing to attack Jericho. He was praying, wondering how to take on such a formidable task. Suddenly, out of nowhere, the Lord appeared.

> Now when Joshua was near Jericho, he looked up and saw a man standing in front of him with a drawn sword in his hand. Joshua went up to him and asked, "Are you for us or for our enemies?" "Neither," he replied, "but

as commander of the army of the Lord I have now come." Then Joshua fell facedown to the ground in reverence, and asked him, "What message does my Lord have for his servant?" (Joshua 5:13, 14).

Face down . . . prostrate . . . like a dead man . . . total surrender describe the safest place on earth to do spiritual battle. When we get vulnerable before the Lord, we are in the right spot to do spiritual warfare.

When I become afraid, unsure of myself, unable to handle the mess I have made of things, I cry out in despair, "Daddy!" And my heavenly Daddy drops what He is doing and rushes in to save me.

My earthly father died when I was young. He was much too young to die, but bad genetics, improper diet and exercise, smoking, and the absence of today's medical advances contributed to his early death. One thing I knew for certain about my father was when I cried out to him, nothing meant more than his little boy.

When I was about 4 or 5 years old, we had my uncle's bird dog in our backyard. My dad loved to hunt quail. I am sure the dog was there for an upcoming hunt. I don't remember all the details, but for some reason, Jake, my uncle's bird dog, decided to take me down. I remember looking at him sitting beside the steps. The next thing I knew he was on top of me with my head almost totally in his mouth. I could almost hear the scraping sound of his teeth on my skull. I screamed like any child would. Looking straight up, all I could see was the mouth and throat of that dog. But, out of my peripheral vision, I saw my father rushing in with a Tonka toy in his right hand. The toy swung swift and sure and the dog lost his grip. One swipe of his hand and my father had beaten back the attacker and delivered me.

David said God had done the same thing for him in Psalms: "I sought the Lord, and he answered me; he delivered me from all my fears" (34:4). "For you, O Lord, have delivered my soul from death, my eyes from tears, my feet from stumbling" (116:8).

Actually, the psalmist describes exactly what needs to take place in our churches today. It's really simple. We need God!

> May God arise, may his enemies be scattered; may his foes flee before him. As smoke is blown away by the wind, may you blow them away; as wax melts before the fire, may the wicked perish before God (68:1, 2).

We need God to stand up once more and exert His mighty power. While I have no trouble with some people trying to identify and pray against the ruling principality or power in their city, I do know this: *When Father stands up, it doesn't matter who the ruling demon is!*

To shout and proclaim a prophetic word in the face of demonic powers sounds great, but when Daddy hears the cries of His oppressed children and comes running, it really doesn't matter what their names are. When He shows up, there is no contest.

Are people hungry for deliverance? Let me pose a simple question: "Were you?" When you were enslaved, trapped, unable to extricate yourself from the bondage that held you fast, did you want to be free? Are you glad you are free now? While there are many who don't want anything to do with the freedom offered by Jesus Christ, there are millions waiting for the church to enter the battle against the power of the Enemy so they can be set free. I think people will join that kind of church. Can we become such a place remains the pressing question.

Brothers, I could not address you as spiritual but as worldly—mere infants in Christ. I gave you milk, not solid food, for you were not yet ready for it. Indeed, you are still not ready. You are still worldly. For since there is jealousy and quarreling among you, are you not worldly? Are you not acting like mere men? For when one says, "I follow Paul," and another, "I follow Apollos," are you not mere men? What, after all, is Apollos? And what is Paul? Only servants, through whom you came to believe—as the Lord has assigned to each his task. I planted the seed, Apollos watered it, but God made it grow. So neither he who plants nor he who waters is anything, but only God, who makes things grow. The man who plants and the man who waters have one purpose, and each will be rewarded according to his own labor. For we are God's fellow workers; you are God's field, God's building (1 Corinthians 3:1-9).

6

A Working Church

The problems Paul addresses in the Corinthian church are still prevalent today. We choose to ignore them and take on larger issues, but the same predicaments that created havoc in the Corinthian church hinder us centuries later.

For instance, they had to deal with worldly attitudes and nasty snipings within their fellowship. Factions developed over, of all things, which preacher each group liked best. Of course, we don't have that problem today with all the television and radio preachers who preach exactly the same thing!

One preacher will tell you how filthy rich you are supposed to be, followed by another preacher denouncing wealth as being of the devil. Flip the channel or drive down the street and you can find someone telling you all sickness is of Satan. He will be followed by someone else encouraging you to tough it out anytime you are ill. The fact is, you can find someone who will support your point of view regardless of the issue.

I think the best advice we can give today is to get into the Word of God—I mean really get into the Word, sift through the myriad of teachings and come to some bedrock truth. That's what Paul was trying to accomplish with this letter to the Corinthians. He wanted them to grow up and become strong men and women of God.

He called upon them to stop acting like "mere men," and start acting like the sons and daughters of God they really were. For that to happen, they had to come to grips with the fact that whatever men do, whatever methods or machinery they use, it is God working with them that produces results. That's the gist of Paul's wisdom—men plant, but God makes it grow.

However, Paul goes on to make a profound statement that applies to us. In verse 9, Paul gives us a job description—something many of us don't really want to hear. He says *God expects us to work in His kingdom!* The same verse says, "For we are God's fellow workers; you are God's field, God's building."

Paul says you and I are God's "fellow workers." This verse and several others in the New Testament highlight our responsibility. As crazy as this may sound, God expects us to produce for Him. Notice other places this term is used:

Greet Priscilla and Aquila, my fellow workers in Christ Jesus (Romans 16:3).

Timothy, my fellow worker, sends his greetings to you, as do Lucius, Jason and Sosipater, my relatives (v. 21).

As for Titus, he is my partner and fellow worker among you; as for our brothers, they are representatives of the churches and an honor to Christ (2 Corinthians 8:23).

A quick study of these verses reveals what Paul meant by the term *fellow worker*. Those people he listed assisted him in his ministry. Without them, he would not have been as productive for God. That's what fellow workers are all about. Working together, fellow workers can do some powerful things.

Here's something really amazing to contemplate: *There are things God wants done that cannot be done apart from partnership with men!*

- God is powerful, but He is not going to teach a Sunday school class.

- God is awesome, but He is not going to lead a ministry that cares for the shut-in.

- God is wonderful, but He is not going to carry the message of the gospel to the lost.

- God is marvelous, but He is not going to raise funds to carry on world missions.

God depends on people like you and me to do the work of the Kingdom, and if we don't do it, it won't get done!

113

Time-on-the-Floor Disease

Pentecostals and Charismatics love to experience the moving of the Holy Spirit. We delight in a powerful move of God that leaves us utterly dazzled. People who are not familiar with the practice probably think we are crazy. Those who love a move of the Spirit are totally comfortable laying before the Lord. We love to be "slain in the Spirit." We love to be caught up in the glory of God and experience His fresh winds.

Actually, if you are at all like me, you are addicted to this kind of worship. We just can't get enough of the presence of the Lord. We buy books, listen to tapes, drive long distances—whatever it takes to have a fresh encounter with God.

Many of us have had a wonderful, personal Pentecost. And I must admit, that's a great place to live. The problem is, God never intended for us to live in that state of euphoria. He means for us to take that anointing—that glory—and go to work in His vineyard.

But thousands of us have developed a terrible case of "time on the floor disease." We like basking in the glory of the Holy Ghost, but we refuse to get up. We like the touch of God we received six years ago, but we have forgotten God gave us that blessing so we could bless others!

It's time we get up off the floor and go to work. I wonder how many times we are going to have to be prayed for and slain in the Spirit before we understand God is calling us to a place of service in His field. How many times are we going to rush off to another revival service, eager to experience the glory of God, only to miss one more time the call of the Father to work for Him?

Why Don't We Work for God?

It's time we addressed some difficult questions. The statistics are pretty much true that say 20 percent of the people in any church are doing 80 percent of the work. What are the rest of us doing for the Lord? Why do churches appear full of people who never do anything for the Lord? Why are so few of us involved in ministry?

Perhaps dealing with some common excuses will assist us in getting involved in God's work.

1. *One reason many of us don't do anything for God centers around our lack of passion for the Lord and compassion for others.* I am afraid many of us have taken the same path God's people did in ancient Israel.

> You have forgotten God your Savior; you have not remembered the Rock, your fortress. Therefore, though you set out the finest plants and plant imported vines, though on the day you set them out, you make them grow, and on the morning when you plant them, you bring them to bud, yet the harvest will be as nothing in the day of disease and incurable pain (Isaiah 17:10, 11).

Does a maiden forget her jewelry, a bride her wedding

ornaments? Yet my people have forgotten me, days without number (Jeremiah 2:32).

In you men accept bribes to shed blood; you take usury and excessive interest and make unjust gain from your neighbors by extortion. And you have forgotten me, declares the Sovereign Lord (Ezekiel 22:12).

May we stop and remember that we were nothing when God found us and raised us up. We owe the Lord everything, not just a tithe or an offering—everything! If there is one thing we should be passionate about, it's loving our God!

I know many people who get all worked up about how good the Lord has been to them, but they couldn't care less about someone else who needs God's love. We need a fresh baptism of compassion for lost men and women in the church today!

When you stop to think about it, we have become so inoculated by statistics, we are scarcely moved when we hear the following statistics:

- In the United States, some 2 million people die every year; yet only about 200,000 know Jesus as their personal Savior.[1]

- Today, approximately 178 million Americans are fundamentally unchurched.

- In this country, we close about 3,500 churches every year.

- Only China and India have more unchurched people than the United States.

It's time for us to stop being in the hazy cloud of God's glory and get to work in His kingdom. It's time for us to place our feet in the tear-soaked steps of Jesus.

He stood on the hillside and looked down on the city of God. Knowing what was going to happen to Him, He wept over them. The pathos in His voice still echoes today.

"O Jerusalem, Jerusalem, you who kill the prophets and stone those sent to you, how often I have longed to gather your children together, as a hen gathers her chicks under her wings, but you were not willing" (Matthew 23:37).

But Jesus did more than stand there and cry. He went forth and labored, laying down His life, for the salvation of that city—for you and me as well. May God touch us today and fill us with so much passion for Him and compassion for others that we cannot help but step forward and serve Him with reckless abandon!

2. *Another reason so many of us don't work for God is our consumer mentality.* We view the church solely as a place to have our own needs met, rather than as a place where we can lay our lives down in sacrificial service to Jesus. We have created a generation of nitpicky consumers who sneer at the slightest inconvenience, rather than become a band of red-hot zealots for God who will make any sacrifice needed to advance the kingdom of God. Face it, many of us have become "consumers" rather than "crusaders."

Our whole intent on Sunday is to find a way God can

bless *me* or to discover a truth that will enhance *my* lifestyle. A huge percentage of us never think about bringing the lost with us so they can hear the gospel and be saved.

This must change if we are to survive and do the work of God. A whole new generation of men and women must arise and begin to serve the Lord with fervor and abandon. It's the only chance we have of lighting this dark world.

It hurts to hear this, and some will vehemently disagree with my spin on the Scripture, but God calls us not to be shoppers, but soldiers.

- A shopper looks around for the best bargain, the most exciting show going; a soldier plunges headlong into battle because he is under orders.

- A shopper complains and whines about virtually everything; a soldier keeps his complaints to himself and does his duty.

- A shopper will stay home if it is too hot, too cold, raining, or he just doesn't feel like going; a soldier marches to battle in spite of pain and depravation.

God has called each of you to sacrificially lay your life on the altar before Him and serve Him with all your might. His Word tells us, "And anyone who does not carry his cross and follow me cannot be my disciple" (Luke 14:27). "Endure hardship with us like a good soldier of Christ Jesus" (2 Timothy 2:3).

Cross bearing and soldiering mark the life of the Christian. It's time to stop our shopping excursions and get into the battle for souls.

3. *Some people won't work for God because they don't feel they are good enough.* Somehow we have fostered the idea that God only uses those who reach a certain level of perfection. At least that's what I used to think. I would look at someone—most of the time it was my pastor—and think to myself, *Wow, I could never live so close to God. He is perfect!* I developed that false image by only coming into contact with those leaders on limited occasions and in controlled circumstances. Most of the time, they were preaching and I was dazzled by their skills in the pulpit.

Over time, I was able to get a little closer to them. When I did, I made a startling discovery—they struggled just like I do, with some of the same issues I have! Then, I came to a revelation that some of you who are afraid you are not good enough for God to use also need to discover this truth: *the grace of God is greater than my hangups!*

God is a Master at taking broken, banged-up vessels and using them for His glory. After all, that's all He has to work with! Paul made an astounding statement in 2 Corinthians 4:7: "But we have this treasure in jars of clay to show that this all-surpassing power is from God and not from us."

119

You pick out the very best and they are nothing more than clay pots—imperfect, rough, fragile. None of us are stainless steel vessels, perfectly formed with no rough edges or indestructible. We all have faults and tendencies that lean toward breaking.

God designed it that way so the glory would all be His. The treasure is not the pot, it's what the pot holds! God has placed within each of you a valuable treasure. He wants to pour that treasure out on the people around you, but He can't until you are willing to be broken and poured out.

If you are going to wait until you "get it all together" or feel like you are perfect before you give yourself to the Lord in service, you will be an old, shriveled-up, dried-out skeleton sitting on a pew. God can, and will, use imperfect vessels in His kingdom. After all, He has used many in the past and since that's all He has today, He will keep blessing the earth through men and women who have fault lines in their lives.

The Issue of Time

Some people will tell you the main reason they can't be involved in ministry is time, or a lack of it. I don't buy that. We find the time to do the things we want to do. It's a problem with our priorities that keeps us from giving time to God.

The time issue before us is much more pressing than

finding an hour to invest in teaching a class or leading a boy's ministry in a midweek service. We are running out of time to do the work of God. If we could only see how close we are to the end of the Biblical term, *last days*, we would probably stop doing everything not essential to survival, and devote every waking moment possible to the kingdom of God.

Yes, time is running out. Jesus warned us of the impending passing of time and the inability of men to work in His kingdom. "As long as it is day, we must do the work of him who sent me. Night is coming, when no one can work" (John 9:4).

Paul took the same time frame and described it differently. Rather than looking at things from the standpoint of the worker using every moment of available daylight to labor, he took the perspective of the saint struggling against the darkness of this evil world who was anticipating the day when the Lord would come. "The night is nearly over; the day is almost here. So let us put aside the deeds of darkness and put on the armor of light" (Romans 13:12).

Either way you look at it, the results are exactly the same. When all is said and done, the believer is in heaven with God and the lost are in deep trouble, awaiting judgment and hell.

Jesus put an exclamation mark at the end of the sentence when He gave us these parting words through

John: "Behold, I am coming soon! My reward is with me, and I will give to everyone according to what he has done" (Revelation 22:12).

You may argue that many centuries have passed since that utterance, thus it is an invalid statement. I take the opposite position. The passage of so much time means His coming is upon us. If I tell you I am coming over to your house and I am going to do it in a hurry, the fact that a few minutes have passed does not mean I am not coming. It means the time when I will knock on your door is imminently approaching with each passing minute. So it is with the coming of our Lord. We simply don't have the time we used to have.

I know that some people no longer believe in the second coming of Jesus. It's a fairy tale to them. They are looking for the Antichrist, the Tribulation and the Kingdom to come and take over the earth. You name it, people are looking for it. If you are one of those who does not believe Jesus could come back any moment . . . fine. You are still running out of time!

There is more to this urgency we need to feel than *hearing the trumpet*—much more. While it is true that there may be some passing of time before we hear the trumpet, every day that passes brings some people to a place where they become so hardened it is difficult, if not impossible, to reach them with the love of God.

☼ There are children in our cities who will witness

things and have atrocities happen to them that will harden them so that they will reject the gospel unless a dedicated worker tells them of the love of God.

⌂ There are young people who can still be reached, if we will work hard enough. If not, they will die from an overdose or spend their lives battling a drug habit that could have been avoided if they had known the liberating power of Christ

⌂ There are businesspeople whose lives are so messed up they are open to the gospel right now. However, in a few months, they will have made such horrific mistakes that makes them totally withdraw and become the people living under a bridge or take their own lives because of the disgrace.

For those people, it's not hearing the trumpet—it's the hardened heart. It's the stony rejection of truth because their lives have become so calloused, so flinty and hard, they will not listen to you. For the sake of those men, women, boys and girls, we must rise up and realize time is running out.

Another group for whom time is short has nothing to do with hearing the trumpet or hardening the heart. It has everything to do with a *failure of health*. People are dying all around us. I mentioned earlier that some 2 million people die in America every year, yet only about 200,000 of them know Jesus. That's about 1 in 10. You can find out how many people in your city or county die every year and figure out just how many souls slip into hell from your area every year.

Where I live (Mobile, Alabama) there were 43,258 deaths in 1997.[2] If the earlier statistics are accurate, that means that 38,932 people in 1997 slipped into a Christless eternity. Nearly 39,000 people who lived within driving range of my church are destined to spend eternity in hell!

You may argue that I live in the Bible Belt and the statistics are out of line because of the dense population of believers in the South. Even if one half of those who died were dedicated believers, that would mean that nearly 22,000 people who live around my church died and went to hell in 1997!

Time Is Running Out!

If Jesus tarries another hundred years, there will be those whose health will fail because of a disease, an accident or some form of violence next week, next month, next year. It is imperative that we work feverishly to save as many as possible before time runs out.

One of my favorite movies is titled *When Worlds Collide*. It's one of those late '50s movies based on a great novel by Edwin Balmer and Philip Wylie. Toward the end of the movie, time is running out. The earth is going to be destroyed in just a few days. As the workers frantically scramble to assemble the gigantic space ark that will hopefully take a few of them to a new world, a voice comes booming over the sound of construction. It urges them to hurry. They are behind schedule. Time is of the essence. Time to waste is not available.

Materials mean nothing. Money means nothing. Saving the scrap from a piece of steel that has been cut with a torch means nothing. Taking time to tidy up the launching pad and dress up the entire area with landscaping is not important. All those things we think are so vital today mean nothing when time is running out.

I am convinced Jesus will supply all the materials we need if we will just get busy doing His work. He will take care of all those things that will become trivial one day after He has come back. But we must become zealous for His kingdom and put Him first in our lives.

The world is looking for just such a place to find God. Could it be the church could get so immersed in serving Jesus that they could find Him here?

Since we live by the Spirit, let us keep in step with the Spirit. Let us not become conceited, provoking and envying each other. Brothers, if someone is caught in a sin, you who are spiritual should restore him gently. But watch yourself, or you also may be tempted. Carry each other's burdens, and in this way you will fulfill the law of Christ. If anyone thinks he is something when he is nothing, he deceives himself (Galatians 5:25—6:3).

A Caring Church

T hose who study statistics and raw numbers, inform us that by the time we go to bed tonight, eight Christian churches in America will close their doors for good. As we drift off to sleep, some 7,600 professing believers in North America and Europe will have left the Christian church for good, deciding the church no longer meets their needs.

These numbers mean nothing, unless one of the eight churches closing down happens to be yours. And 7,600 people is a drop in the bucket, unless four of those happen to be your son, daughter-in-law and two grandchildren who are walking away from the only hope of eternity. When it hits close to home, we get excited and demand that someone do something, even if it's wrong.

The only hope we have of surviving the days to come is to become a church that cares—genuinely cares—for people. And, since the pew couldn't care less who sits on it and the sound system is not at all picky about who listens; since the doors do not have an opinion about who opens them and the color of the carpet doesn't stand up and demand that only certain people walk on it . . . *the caring church consists of caring people!*

Paul was trying to get that message across to those saints in the Galatian church. Spirit-filled living, in its purest form, is caring for those around you. It's grabbing your brother and sister by the arm and encouraging them to press on, affirming them in the truth that they can make it.

I heard the story of a young lady named Linda who was traveling alone in a rundown Honda Civic on the rough highway from Alberta to the Yukon. That's tough country, usually reserved for leathery men and monstrous four-wheel-drive vehicles. She wanted to get an early start, so she asked for a 5 o'clock wake-up call.

Rising early, she was greeted by the impenetrable fog and had to wait. Going into a small diner, she was asked by two rather large men who were truck drivers, "Where are you headed?" She told them and they started yelling, "No way! That pass is dangerous in this kind of weather." But she insisted on going through. The men then said, "OK, I guess we will have to hug you."

Linda backed off, indignant at their brazen suggestion. Later she realized they meant putting a truck in the lead and one following behind. So, Linda made it safely to her destination by following the tiny red lights in front of her and with the reassurance of a great power right behind her.[1]

If the apostle Paul were here today, I think he would tell my church, and probably your church, "There are people in your midst who need a hug!" He wouldn't be talking about putting your arms around someone to make him or her feel better, although that is wonderful. No, he would be telling us there are people within the ranks of our fellowship who need someone to help them make it to their final destination.

That's what he told the church at Rome: "We who are strong ought to bear with the failings of the weak and not to please ourselves. Each of us should please his neighbor for his good, to build him up" (15:1, 2).

God wants some to get in front of others and lead the way. He expects some of us to take the point position and forge ahead, calling others to follow all the way into glory.

Everybody Needs Care

Take a moment to consider what Paul really said to that church and to us. Living in step with the Spirit means we care for people, we help them deal with their sins, we help bear their burdens. This type of life fulfills the law of Christ to perfection.

Paul talked about two kinds of Christians in the

passage from Galatians: those struggling and those succeeding. Those struggling appear to be in need of a hug.
They need someone to come alongside and lift them up.
Paul calls for the church to restore that person. The word
restore was used to describe the mending of a net. When
the net was torn, it wasn't thrown away, it was mended
and made fresh. That's what God wants us to do with
someone who is caught in sin.

Sadly, in many churches, someone whose sin becomes
public is not restored—he or she is roasted. The well-
worn cliche has more truth than we would like to admit:
*The church is the only institution on earth that shoots its
wounded.* That's not how it is supposed to be. The
church is called to be a community of the caring. It is
called to be the community of understanding.

One of my pastoral stints placed me within a couple of
miles of the two largest Pentecostal\Charismatic churches in Alabama. Both churches were successful in attract-
ing a large number of believers. One church in particular
held forth a stance about sickness that was tough on anyone who was trying to live faithfully for the Lord, but
who still came down with an illness. Not long after arriv-
ing as pastor, I was called to the hospital to visit a man
who was undergoing cancer surgery. He and his family
were dedicated believers, but they were really crushed by
the stance taken by their church when it was revealed
that he had cancer and in all probability would die.

In time they came to our church where we prayed for him, fasted for him and did everything we knew to do to see him healed. We raised money to send him to Chicago for what was at that time an experimental treatment . . . all to no avail. Two years later, he went home to be with Jesus.

Why did he leave a much larger church with better music, programs, preaching, fellowship? He found his way to us because we cared; we "hugged" a struggling saint and stayed right with him until he made it safely home. That's what church is all about!

Of course, Paul also talked about people who were succeeding. He warned those who were sailing along smoothly to beware, lest they fall prey to the snares of the Enemy. Sometimes our pride about how good we are doing leads to our downfall. More than one of us has "risen to the top," only to discover the pinnacle is simply too small for us to stand on.

Here's what's important: struggling or succeeding, we all need someone to help us!

Satan's Plan

He has a tactic developed just for you. Regardless of the size of your Christian experience, the power of your prayer life, the amount of anointing that oozes from your pores, *Satan has a plan for you!*

The words of the apostle Peter have never been more

appropriate than today: "Be self-controlled and alert. Your enemy the devil prowls around like a roaring lion looking for someone to devour" (1 Peter 5:8).

Anyone who knows about lions is aware that they slip up on a herd and stampede them. By so doing, they can single out the weak, young, or otherwise defenseless member of the herd. That makes killing much easier.

Not long ago I happened to catch a short portion of a documentary about lions. To my amazement, a pride of young lions had a large hippo cornered. You may think hippos are stupid, defenseless beasts. Far from it. More people are killed in Africa every year by hippos than by any other animal. They are dangerous, quick, ill-tempered, powerful beasts with skin like armor. After all, if you make your living in crocodile-infested waters and make those monster lizards give way when you come around, you have to be pretty tough.

But this hippo was in trouble. The lions would jump on his back and try to bring him down. He would turn and snap his mighty jaws. What struck me was his size. He could have taken one of those full-grown lions into his mouth and had room to spare! But here he was, in trouble with the lions. I didn't see the entire program, so I don't know if he made it to safety or not. If he did, he surely had some scars to show after the battle.

That scene really disturbed me because I saw more than a brutal scene being carried out on the African savanna. I saw a spiritual principle being played out in a natural setting. Many of us have taken on the aura of the hippo—tough, independent, aloof, powerful, able to fend off any attack, able to take it—only to discover to our shock that the Enemy of our soul had a plan devised just for us!

It really doesn't matter how strong you are, how many times you have survived, how long you have been a Christian, Satan has a plan designed for you. And he is relentless. He's just waiting for the right moment to attack. If he can catch you out there by yourself, you don't have a chance! And if by chance you do make it back, you will definitely have scars to show for your wandering!

That's why we need a church that cares. We must follow fast after the admonition of the Word of God in Acts 2:40: "With many other words he warned them; and he pleaded with them, "Save yourselves from this corrupt generation.""

On the Day of Pentecost, the apostle Peter *pleaded* with them to be saved. He went beyond an attitude that said, "Take it or leave it." He pressed in to encourage them to come to Christ. That's the attitude we must take in order to see people saved today.

But encouragement went further than just getting people saved. It spilled over into the fellowship of the redeemed. This theme seems to dominate the teachings of the New Testament to the point that once a person has been saved, there is hardly anything more important than to encourage one another.

> And we urge you, brothers, warn those who are idle, encourage the timid, help the weak, be patient with everyone (1 Thessalonians 5:14).

> Preach the Word; be prepared in season and out of season; correct, rebuke and encourage—with great patience and careful instruction (2 Timothy 4:2).

> But encourage one another daily, as long as it is called Today, so that none of you may be hardened by sin's deceitfulness (Hebrews 3:13).

People in churches all across America (actually around the world) will walk out and stumble into the snare Satan has set for them if someone doesn't reach out and touch them for Christ,

- A single parent who has gone through a messy divorce will walk out thinking no one cares if you don't show him or her love.
- A young person might decide it's just too easy to give in to drugs and alcohol if you don't share with him or her the strength to stand.
- A businessman may just decide to go ahead and have that affair if he doesn't somehow gain strength from some brothers who give him a "hug."
- Some struggling saints might just drop out and

slip away discouraged—never to return—if you don't embrace them and let them know you care.

Eternity hangs in the balance for people today and *you* hold the keys! Most people in the church world are not familiar with the name Andrew Meekin. I came across his story some years ago in Greg Laurie's book, *The Upside Down Church*. Andrew was on a plane that was hijacked. When the hijackers bungled their plans and there was not enough fuel to get to their destination, the pilot announced he was going to crash-land the jet in the ocean.

Can you imagine the chaos and terror that ensued? Andrew was a member of the Evangelical Church in Addis Ababa, the capital of Ethiopia. He wasn't a preacher; he was a man who loved God and was on his way to a Bible conference. When the grim news was announced, Andrew stood up and presented the gospel of Jesus Christ over the shouts and cries of terror. He invited the people to respond. A flight attendant who survived stated that 20 people accepted his invitation and received Jesus as Savior a few moments prior to their death.[2]

Courageous? You better believe it! Exciting? Few things will ever equal it for excitement! Daring? It was on the edge for sure! But every one of us faces that exact scenario every time we gather in the house of God. There are people all around us whose "planes" are going down.

⌂ The financial pressure is killing them.

⸎ Their marriage is like a shot-up plane leaking oil. It's a slow, painful crash waiting to happen.

⸎ The hectic pace of life has caught up with them and they can no longer cope.

⸎ The faith they once leaned on has grown weak because of lack of nourishment and they are limping along, about to fall away.

⸎ They once worshiped God with us, but we just haven't seen them in a long time.

May God raise up some "Andrew Meekins" in the local church who, understanding the dynamics of the day in which we live, will stand up and rescue the perishing before it is too late. They are here! They walk among us every weekend! They come in and out of our fellowships, locked in a desperate search for someone who will care. *O God, pour out a spirit of compassion on Your church this day!*

Minding My Own Business

Many of us have decided the safest thing to do is to stand around and just mind our own business. You know, take care of "me and mine" and not get involved with the messy situations of other people's lives.

That sounds good, unless we take the Bible seriously. If we take the Word of God at face value, we cannot dispense with our duty, our calling, to help our brothers and sisters on the journey to heaven.

Actually, a close examination of Paul's command to

the Galatian church can be troubling, if we want to just mind our own business. "Carry each other's burdens, and in this way you will fulfill the law of Christ" (6:2).

The word he used for *carry* means "to lift something off." It comes from a root word meaning "to walk." It does no injustice to Paul's writing to say we are to *lift the burden off our brother as we walk along with him.* If I am to accomplish that task, I have to be involved with you, traveling the same path.

God takes a rather dim view of those who just stand around and mind their own business. Look at what the Lord said to Edom about this issue:

"Because of the violence against your brother Jacob, you will be covered with shame; you will be destroyed forever. On the day you stood aloof while strangers carried off his wealth and foreigners entered his gates and cast lots for Jerusalem, you were like one of them" (Obadiah 10, 11).

Edom was a descendant of Esau. Of course, Esau and Jacob were brothers. These people stood by and minded their own business when the Babylonians invaded and eventually sacked Israel. They actually pillaged some of the area when the invaders backed off. It wasn't that the Edomites, the relatives of the Israelites, actually killed them. They just stood by and did nothing while the enemy executed their brothers. This disgusting thing brought God's wrath on their heads.

137

I do not wish to overspiritualize the message of Obadiah, but I am convinced that there are parallels to our day. I think we can become "Edomites" in the sense that we simply "stand around and mind our own business" while the Enemy launches his well-planned schemes on our relatives in Christ.

If I understand the thrust of Obadiah's words, to stand by and watch while the Enemy rakes my brother or sister over the coals is the same in God's eyes, as joining in and making the fire hotter! To just stand around and watch them go under because of their heavy load is tantamount to adding to the load and making their way more difficult. It just may be that those who were so careful not to offend others out of a fear of causing someone to stumble and fall will have to answer anyway because they failed to alleviate the pain of a hurting brother or sister. May God awaken us and make us burden bearers!

Finding Fish and Shepherding Sheep

In one of the final conversations between the resurrected Jesus and the restored apostle Peter, Jesus directed the strong-willed fisherman in a direction he was not very comfortable traveling. The conversation is found in John 21.

When they had finished eating, Jesus said to Simon Peter, "Simon son of John, do you truly love me more than these?" "Yes, Lord," he said, "you know that I love you." Jesus said, "Feed my lambs." Again Jesus said, "Simon son of John, do you truly love me?" He answered, "Yes, Lord, you know that I love you." Jesus said, "Take care of my sheep." The third time he said to him, "Simon son of John, do you love me?" Peter was hurt because Jesus asked him the third time, "Do you love me?" He said, "Lord, you know all things; you know that I love you." Jesus said, "Feed my sheep. I tell you the truth, when you were younger you dressed yourself and went where you wanted; but when you are old you will stretch out your hands, and someone else will dress you and lead you where you do not want to go." Jesus said this to indicate the kind of death by which Peter would glorify God. Then he said to him, "Follow me!" Peter turned and saw that the disciple whom Jesus loved was following them. [This was the one who had leaned back against Jesus at the supper and had said, "Lord, who is going to betray you?"] When Peter saw him, he asked, "Lord, what about him?" Jesus answered, "If I want him to remain alive until I return, what is that to you? You must follow me" (vv. 15-22).

Peter was a fisherman. When he was first called to follow Jesus, the message was couched in talk a fisherman would grasp. Jesus came by while Peter and his brother Andrew were fishing. The Lord called out, "Come, follow me . . . and I will make you fishers of men!" (Mark 1:17). He left the nets that day, but fishing was a subject he understood.

Now, on the eve of the inauguration of the church age, Jesus switches gears and starts all this shepherding talk.

Three times He tells the renewed apostle, "Feed my sheep!" It apparently got to Peter because he finally looked around at John and, no doubt trying to shift the focus off his life, inquired about the job description the Lord had for John. Jesus promptly said, "None of your business! You just do what I told you—be a shepherd to my sheep!"

Catching men is vital. Getting men saved is vital, but so is keeping them. Jesus was fastidious about keeping that which God gave. He was so meticulous about it, they gathered 12 baskets of food from the tiny lunch after the Lord had fed thousands. Think about it . . . tons of food available and Jesus makes them pick up scraps!

While I would never belittle anyone, I do want all to know this truth: *You may consider yourself a tiny scrap of bread sitting next to a filet mignon, but you are so important to Jesus that He started the whole church dispensation by telling the greatest fisherman of all time, "Take care of the sheep!"*

Each of us is so important to Jesus that He calls the entire church to care. He also promises sure punishment to anyone who just stands around while others falter and fall by the wayside.

Oh yes, both God and the world are looking for a church that cares. The world is searching to find a place to be loved, a place that will make a difference in their lives. God is looking for a church He can trust to deposit

His treasure in so it will be well cared for. I guess the pressing question is, "Are we a church that cares?"

Say what we want, the answer becomes evident as time goes by. My prayer is that we will become such a caring community that men and women will run to us with their needs and we can bring God and humanity together so something great can happen.

In Damascus there was a disciple named Ananias. The Lord called to him in a vision, "Ananias!" "Yes, Lord," he answered. The Lord told him, "Go to the house of Judas on Straight Street and ask for a man from Tarsus named Saul, for he is praying. In a vision he has seen a man named Ananias come and place his hands on him to restore his sight." "Lord," Ananias answered, "I have heard many reports about this man and all the harm he has done to your saints in Jerusalem. And he has come here with authority from the chief priests to arrest all who call on your name." But the Lord said to Ananias, "Go! This man is my chosen instrument to carry my name before the Gentiles and their kings and before the people of Israel. I will show him how much he must suffer for my name." Then Ananias went to the house and entered it. Placing his hands on Saul, he said, "Brother Saul, the Lord—Jesus, who appeared to you on the road as you were coming here—has sent me so that you may see again and be filled with the Holy Spirit." Immediately, something like scales fell from Saul's eyes, and he could see again. He got up and was baptized, and after taking some food, he regained his strength. Saul spent several days with the disciples in Damascus. At once he began to preach in the synagogues that Jesus is the Son of God (Acts 9:10-20).

8

A Willing Church

I sn't it amazing how stuck in the mud the church can become? Have you ever stopped to think about how intransigent we get over things which, in the scope of eternity, really don't matter? I have no intention of quoting statistics. We have already heard enough sobering news to startle us with this fact: *the church, as we know it, is in deep trouble.*

Our days of influencing society and enforcing moral codes from our ivory towers are over. The world either ignores us or takes up arms of aggression against us. I am convinced that our failure to move on with God—to abandon our "fortress mentality" and seek a fresh revelation from God about how we are to do ministry—will be our undoing.

A statement made by Peter F. Drucker in his book *Managing the Non-Profit Organization* sounds so much like a prophetic word, it alarms me. His declaration? In a discussion concerning moving with the times, he says, "Things that were of primary importance may become secondary or even totally irrelevant. You must watch this constantly, or else very soon you will become a museum piece."[1]

That's upsetting. It shouts at me that I cannot depend on things remaining the way they were. The church cannot rest on accomplishments of the past and simply think God is always going to be there just because He was there in days gone by.

God moves. He lives. He is fluid. While always the same in nature, character and commitment, God is forever changing the way He accomplishes His divine purpose. If we, the church, fail to seek His face and remain in the up-to-date flow of His anointing, we will indeed become nothing more than museums where people point to the works of men long dead. May God awaken us. May His Holy Spirit once again breathe fire into our lives and revive our churches. May we know Him once more as the living, awesome God.

A New Direction

How would you have liked to have been Ananias? Poor guy. He was minding his own business, loving God and doing his best to adjust to the persecution being perpetrated by this Pharisee named Saul. One day, the Lord spoke to him and said, "Ananias, I have a job for you." Ananias, being a good servant, said, "Sure, Lord, anything for You." The Lord said, "Saul is over in a house on Straight Street belonging to a guy named Judas. Go over there and pray for him" (see Acts 9:10-19).

Can you imagine how bad that sounded? First of all, he is going to the house of a man named Judas. I ask you, could there be a worse name to have had in the first-century church than Judas?

On top of that, he is to go and pray for Saul. Talk about a new direction for a settled church. This is going to mess things up royally. At this point, everyone knows who everyone is. You don't need a program. Simon Peter and his bunch are the good guys. Saul and his bunch are the bad guys, and Saul is the "baddest" of them all. Now, God wants to rearrange the players and Ananias is called to be the talent scout.

No one could have blamed him if he had said, "No!" Saul was killing Christians like Ananias. Saul was imprisoning people like Ananias. Why put it all on the line for a man like that?

Think about it for a moment. Up to this point in the Acts narrative, how had people been won to Christ? Things followed a fairly predictable pattern:

- There would be a great miracle or series of healings.
- Someone, usually the apostle Peter, would stand and preach the message of Jesus.

⚘ People would be saved and then baptized.

Sounds like a nice program, but you weren't going to win Saul of Tarsus with that program. Miracles were not going to move him, and you certainly weren't going to argue him into the fold. This is where many churches and denominations have lost their edge. They have decided on a "one size fits all" method that no longer fits. Rather than moving on with God and following Him, they are hung up on how they used to do things.

That nicely settled church had to move outside the established comfort zone to win this guy named Saul. What's really great about the story is the fact that as soon as they were willing to venture forth with God, the greatest champion of all time was brought into the family of God.

That's what happens when we shake off the bands of tradition and follow the voice of God. He raises up greatness in our midst that is suited for the need of the hour. Saul, whom we now know as Paul, was exactly what was needed in the body of Christ at that time. Ananias didn't know that. The church leadership over in Jerusalem didn't know it either. Neither did the councils that met and determined the order of the church. But God knew. And God was moving the church in a new direction—one that would reach around the world.

Who knows what God wants to raise up among us? Who can know the plan of God for the church in the future? Only this is certain: *Unless we are willing to lay aside our comfortable pattern and follow the winds of the Spirit, God's plan will not be taking place in our little corner.*

Stuck in the Middle With You!

So many in church leadership (pastors, deacons, elders or those in supervision of a group of churches) are finding themselves in precisely the same sticky spot as Samuel did when God wanted to move on in a new direction with David. It's tough! Tough choices have to be made. Choices that are sometimes painful and can even be dangerous. Samuel understood how those who want to follow God feel today. The thrill of knowing you are walking with the Lord is great, but so are the risks. Consider this snippet from the life of Samuel:

> The Lord said to Samuel, "How long will you mourn for Saul, since I have rejected him as king over Israel? Fill your horn with oil and be on your way; I am sending you to Jesse of Bethlehem. I have chosen one of his sons to be king." But Samuel said, "How can I go? Saul will hear about it and kill me." The Lord said, "Take a heifer with you and say, 'I have come to sacrifice to the Lord.' Invite Jesse to the sacrifice, and I will show you what to do. You are to anoint for me the one I indicate" (1 Samuel 16:1-3).

In a revealing scene from the life of this great leader, we discover this amazing fact: Samuel was scared of where the Lord was taking him! Think about it for a moment. Samuel was a man who had heard from the Lord very early on and who had confronted the aged prophet Eli. He had witnessed the death of Eli and the collapse of his rulership in Israel. Over time, he brought the ark back to the proper place of worship. He confronted the Philistines and led the nation. He had overseen the painful transition from following the voice of God through the prophet to the choice of a king—even outlining the conduct of his successor. Samuel had even anointed the new king, confronting him on issues where he was wrong. Now, he was afraid.

God was taking the nation in a new direction. The day of Saul was over and the day of David was on the horizon. Samuel was stuck right in the middle. His choice was to go with Saul and let God move on without him, or risk it all and follow David.

The choices Samuel confronted are similar to the choices we make today.

- Do we stay with what used to work because it is comfortable and we like it? Or do we risk something new because that's what God is blessing?
- Do we zealously hold on to traditions of the past, ignoring the present needs of people, simply because we have elevated our traditions to the level of Scripture?
- Do we decry anyone else having a move of God if it doesn't fit our definition of a "move of God"?

Of course, those are broad swipes of the brush. All across our land, local churches are locked in power struggles trying to determine the direction the body is headed. Some are locked into position on the issues, while others see God moving in a certain area and want to follow what God is blessing. Issues abound, but here are a few:

- Do we sing hymns out of a book or choruses off the wall?
- Do we allow our young people to use music we don't like, or do we limit what God can use to what suits our taste?
- Is it written in stone that Sunday school has to be at 9:45, morning worship at 10:45 and a Sunday evening service held each week?
- Is God really in the "laughing movement" and what happened at Brownsville?

Today, the church stands at a crossroads. We can choose to remain with Saul because, in spite of all his shortcomings, he is familiar and we like some of the things he stands for. Or we can choose to risk it all and follow the new direction the Lord is laying before us.

I don't want to rain on anyone's parade, but this is a new day and God is moving in ways we never thought possible. Let me give you one example. If you are like me, you came along at the very beginning of the technology explosion of the last 25 years. I can remember when everyone was scrambling to purchase an *Atari* game system. You could actually play Ping-Pong on the television screen . . . by yourself! We thought we were in nirvana.

Fast-forward 25 years. Can you imagine giving your child one of those systems for Christmas this year? The new systems, upgraded every year or so, are like space shuttles compared to riding in a covered wagon when compared to those first-generation systems. There is simply no comparison.

Now, move over into the church. Take that 10-year-old kid who loves video games. He is an expert. He can shoot aliens, escape from dungeons, ride the surf, drive the cars with the best of them. He lives in a world of bright images, sleek sounds, vibrant colors and sensory-enhancing gadgets. But when he walks into church, we want to hand him a photocopied piece of paper to color with broken crayons and expect him to sit idly for 45 minutes while we fumble around with the outdated slide show. On Saturday he was in a virtual reality game at the mall and we expect him to be satisfied with gluing some wooden sticks on a plate on Sunday . . . *all because that's what they did for us when we were kids!*

That's just one glimpse into the world in which the church now operates. It's scary. The world no longer cuts the church any slack just because we are a "sacred institution." The world could care less about our "sacredness"—they are dying for relevance. Sadly, many churches are dying right along with them because they grasp ever so tightly to their "Saul style" of worship when singing David is about to take over the kingdom.

It's time for the church to stop arguing over all the junk that means nothing in light of eternity and focus on this one issue: *what we must do to become relevant to our culture and win people to Jesus!*

- If we have to change our style of music to reach a new generation, make some changes!
- If we have to alter the way we run our services to make them more appealing to the lost around us, change!
- If we have to create new times of worship on different days, change!
- If we have to put cotton in our ears so young people can play music louder than we like, buy cotton by the bale—but let's win our youth!
- If we have to spend money to train our teachers how to use modern equipment so our children will be challenged with the gospel in the same way they are challenged to "escape the evil clutches of Nardok the Terrible," spend the money!

You aren't nearly as hung up on things remaining the same as you think you are!

People in church tend to get in a position and never move from that spot. As a matter of fact, the longer a person lives, the more he or she tends to dwell on the past rather than living in the present or getting excited about the possibilities of the future. That malady has killed thousands of churches over the centuries. Unfortunately, we all tend to gravitate to that way of thinking unless it deals with our own personal needs.

Over time, we develop our opinions of what God will and won't do, how God will and won't move, what is really allowable and what is taboo. We drive down tent stakes, build altars to our perceptions of God, and pretty much stay right there. We are, in a word, unmovable.

Someone comes along and offers a fresh view of God—a new way of doing ministry, a new perception of the glory of the Lord—and we are like the Rock of Gibraltar. We aren't budging one inch. Move on with God? Forget it! We have it!

That is, until it concerns our personal failures, or shall I dare say *sins*? When we sin, we are ready to ask God to forgive us and move on. We don't want to hear about it. We are ready to press forward into a new day of God's grace. Praise God we can!

In his book *Gettin' There*, Steve Farrar tells the story of the world's largest bulldozer. The monster machine is made by a company called Komatsu. It is 16 feet tall, 22 feet wide and 41 feet long. It weighs 291,000 pounds and can push almost 250,000 tons. Although it is an engineering marvel, that's not the reason he mentioned the machine. Just north of where he lives in Dallas is a large landfill. They use this huge earthmover to dig a hole, push trash in it and cover up the trash so you won't know what's buried beneath.[2]

Millions of dollars are spent on research and development, production and transportation for a machine that can bury the trash as if it was never there.

What a portrait of what God does with our sin. He spends eternity planning, setting up the millions of scenarios necessary. Then, when the time is just right, Jesus comes along and sheds His blood for our sin. Now, because we trust in Him, our sin is gone—out of sight!

When we sin, we come to our Father and plead for mercy and receive it in abundance.

If we confess our sins, he is faithful and just and will forgive us our sins and purify us from all unrighteousness. If we claim we have not sinned, we make him out to be a liar and his word has no place in our lives. My dear children, I write this to you so that you will not sin. But if anybody does sin, we have one who speaks to the Father in our defense—Jesus Christ, the Righteous One (1 John 1:9—2:2).

He is the atoning sacrifice for our sins, and not only for ours but also for the sins of the whole world. Praise God! We can move on with the Lord even after we have failed! That's great news. Here's some even better news. That same God who forgives you of your sinful failures is ready to pick you and your church up and carry you to new places in His grace and glory. It all depends on your willingness to lay aside those things that have hindered you and pursue Him.

God is doing a great thing in the last days. It doesn't always look like the things God did 100 years ago, and it probably shouldn't. The world has changed dramatically. But the basic needs of people haven't changed one bit, and neither has the answer we possess in Jesus Christ. It's time we stop arguing about the design of the medicine bottle and take the cure to the world. Their eternity and our survival depends on such a course of action.

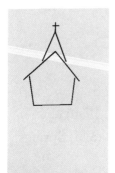 # Endnotes

Chapter 1
[1]Tony Campolo, *The Kingdom of God Is a Party* (Dallas: Word, 1990) 8.

Chapter 2
[1]Eddie Gibbs, *ChurchNext* (Downers Grove: Intervarsity, 2000) 16.
[2]Cited in *Your Church* (May/June, 2001) 8.

Chapter 6
[1]Doug Murren, *Churches That Heal* (West Monroe, LA: Howard, 1999) 104.
[2]Taken from Federal Statistics.

Chapter 7
[1]Jamie Moore, *Experiencing the Joy of Fellowship,* (sermoncentral.com).

[2] Greg Laurie, *The Upside Down Church* (Wheaton: Tyndale, 1999) 62.

Chapter 8

[1]Peter F. Drucker, *Managing the Non-Profit Organization* (New York: HarperCollins, 1990) 6.

[2]Steve Farrar, *Gettin' There* (Colorado Springs: Multnomah, 2001) 78.